THESE
HANDS
I KNOW

Water Song (1985)

some days it's a slow walk to evening (1989)

My Father's Geography (1992)

Stations in a Dream (1993)

Timber and Prayer (1995)

Talisman (1998)

Multitudes: Poems Selected & New (2000)

The Ten Lights of God (2000)

Sandy Point (2000)

These Hands I Know

African-American Writers on Family

Edited by
Afaa Michael Weaver

Sarabande  Books
LOUISVILLE, KENTUCKY

> Managing Editor
> Sarabande Books, Inc.
> 2234 Dundee Road, Suite 200
> Louisville, KY 40205

LIBRARY OF CONGRESS CATALOGING-IN-PUBLICATION DATA

These hands I know : African-American writers on family / edited by Afaa Michael Weaver.
    p.   cm.
  ISBN 1-889330-72-8 (alk. paper)
  1. African-American authors—Family relationships. 2. African-American families. 3. Family—United States.
  I. Weaver, Afaa M. (Afaa Michael), 1951–

PS153.N5 T46 2002
814'.008'0355—dc21   2001054932

Cover image: *Family Dinner, 1968* by Romare Bearden. Collage on paper. © Romare Bearden Foundation / Licensed by VAGA, New York, NY.

Cover and text design by Charles Casey Martin

Manufactured in the United States of America
This book is printed on acid-free paper.

Sarabande Books is a nonprofit literary organization.

Funded in part by a grant from the Kentucky Arts Council, a state agency of the Education, Arts, and Humanities Cabinet

FIRST EDITION

TABLE OF CONTENTS

INTRODUCTION
Sailing to These Shores

Ln his epic poem "Middle Passage," Robert Hayden displays the agony of black families uprooted from Africa, ripped apart by the capitalist industry of selling human beings to other human beings. The dark voyage begins with "sharks following the moans the fever and the dying." The daily rituals of mothers and fathers, daughters, sons, and extended relations become "black gold, black ivory, black seed." Grief and sadness are the cradle of rage, as the Africans travel the Atlantic to America, remembering and forgetting home, and country, in the wash of salt water against wooden vessels; languages and cultures burrowing deep into the safety of the unconscious. Hayden notes the primal energy in the ship holds: "You cannot...kill the deep immortal wish, / the timeless will." Framing the Middle Passage, Hayden gives it this imprimatur: "voyage through death / to life upon these shores." In America, the Africans begin anew to live as families.

Family life is an insistent vessel traveling the space of our struggles to love and to be loved. In *These Hands I Know*, a sparkling host of poets and prose writers reveals the inner workings of African-American families. Some revelations are unabashed, while others are more measured. However, the collection as a whole challenges what has been a cultural rule against revealing our personal business as African-Americans. In assembling these essays, I have come to feel even more firmly that readers should have greater access to literal representations of our inner lives, to further affirmations of the complex lives of people of all cultures, the commonalities that define us all as human beings. Putting one's business in the street is a liberating gesture. One of the ironies of enduring oppression is that the enduring can create its own oppressive energies, namely silence and a belief somehow that every black person possesses an inherent saintliness. The latter can be monstrous.

The common accord of black folk has long been that our private lives are not to be revealed beyond family and community, but Langston Hughes' prophecy of an unashamed poet emerging from the masses has taken the corporeal form of many black poets and writers emerging, a chorus of voices incarnating from the Atlantic's stormy and bloody waves.

Alice Walker is one of those voices, and in *In Search of Our Mothers' Gardens,* she writes honestly of maintaining humanity under the weight of oppression. Acknowledging the effects of white patriarchy on black patriarchy, she notes the one brother who gave her a strong male model, noting also her own directive. "[M]y brothers—except for one—never understood they must represent half the world to me, as I must represent the other half to them." Walker's one brother is an exception to the men in her family, and emblematic of another important truth: White praise of black humanity often offers reverence for the will to survive injustice, but this very praise can turn a blind eye to the individuality of each African-American soul.

Yet we are all individuals, and each of our families is different. Some have more than their share of personal dysfunction; others are more fortunate. That is what is human.

Writing about his boyhood in the early twentieth century,

W. Warren Harper presents another African eye on America, the eye surveying oppression's landscape from a point of self-assuredness. He is the first African-American to make the Catskill High School basketball team. He is conscious, as a young man, of racial struggle, but is not inured to it. His self-image is molded in a proactive and secure response to racism: "I knew I was colored," Harper writes, "but I had never given it any thought."

In more contemporary times, Karen Chandler continues the cultural concern for preparing black children for life in America. In her vigilance for her son's ability to succeed, she has become attuned to a need for vigilance about her own challenges. Chandler writes, "The story of how our society threatens to deny or kill young men's spirits is not new.... Being a mother has meant developing my voice and my confidence more; it's meant being more consistent and open about expressing my will."

The telling of the personal in black family life shows the shifting composition of the African-American community, as black folk from the Caribbean, Africa, and elsewhere establish themselves as Americans. Born in America, Trent Masiki writes of the death and burial of his Ugandan father. Masiki's regrets extend to having to research cultural information he hoped to get from his father, including the function of Abakenekene, the Ugandan subclan to which they belong. It is the group responsible for crowning kings. "His body lay in the city morgue, and if no one claimed it, it would be placed in an unclaimed grave and lost to history."

African-Americans—like anyone else—experience personal trauma within the family, but a trauma that is also complicated by the symbiotic weaving of racism with the familial and personal failures and losses. Honorée Fanonne Jeffers writes of her father's difficulties in teaching at a white university. The academic arrogance and racism transform him from a loving father to an abusive father. The sins of the society are visited on his children through him. As a child, Jeffers wonders what these forces are which find their way into her heart, using her father as a pathway. "Who are these white people who keep me from making him happy?" It is, of course, the racism, but more deeply and tragically perhaps, it is her father's own personal fault lines.

Examining the primal and universal struggles within families, Fred D'Aguiar presents the dynamics in mythic terms. "Father enslaves son. Son hates father, bides his time, waits for the strong father to weaken."

Africans and their descendants in America have always been nothing more and nothing less than human. If anything is constant and universal, it is suffering—personal, social, and political. If these essays offer anything, it is the affirmation of humanity. One of the more difficult aspects of knowing suffering is to know that the exaggeration of one's circumstance—whether good or bad—is just exaggeration, and does not affirm one group's pain to be greater than another's pain. That realization is the crossroads where we have a choice as literary artists and readers. The truth of the interior lives of those of us who are African-Americans is a truth with a vast complexity. However, that can be said of anyone. Hopefully, this collection of essays will offer a view on our times, which is that we have the chance to continue to build anew, by a "voyage through death / to life upon these shores."

Kalamu ya Salaam writes, "We are more than just twisted responses to slavery.... Our insistence on constantly creating family is ideological, not pathological. We believe in the beauty of community."

Afaa Michael Weaver
Sucha Beskidzka, Poland
August, 2001

Henry Louis Gates, Jr.

Up the Hill

When we were growing up, being a Coleman was a very big deal in Piedmont. My uncles and aunts were very well thought of; most went as far at the paper mill as a colored man could go, in their respective trades, once the mill decided to allow blacks out of the loaders. The Colemans were the first colored to own guns and hunt on white land, the first to become Eagle Scouts, the first to go to college, the first to own property.

And at the head of the Coleman clan, when I was young, was Big Mom, my mother's mother, also known as Biggie. She was a figure of reverence and fascination, but most of all, whenever any of her children did not want you to do something, she was a figurative agent of social control.

Big Mom was astoundingly religious. I mean, if there is a Heaven, then Big Mom has *got* to be in it: you can have no doubt about that. Big Mom went to church *every* Sunday. She prayed a lot, and she never went anywhere, at least in my lifetime, except to the doctor and to church. She had started to lose her sight by the time I was a boy, though she could see you close up. Big Mom was always in the kitchen or in the dining room, perched in front of the big picture window that her youngest son, Earkie, had installed when eventually he was allowed to buy Big Mom's house from the Fredlocks, the white people who owned the funeral home over in the Orchard. She called me "Skippy Boy" or "Skipper Ripper Dipper," and spoke with me, rather than merely silently acknowledging another of her nameless, countless grandchildren. And she seemed genuinely to like me, which is the only reason I would have taken all those breathless steps to climb "Up the Hill" to Big Mom's house.

My cousins, my uncountable cousins, all venerated Big Mom, but like "a Virgin Mary image in a church," as Zora Neale Hurston put it. I liked her partly because I could make her laugh. I enjoyed teasing her about running around with Bootsie, or dancing with Mr. Lynn or Mr. Russell down at the colored Legion on Saturday night. She'd laugh real hard at that last one, her bright-pink toothless gums revealed by the pulled-back lips of her laughter. She didn't wear her teeth around the house, saved them for church or the doctor's. I'd push up against the limits, the boundaries of the allowable things for a devilish grandson to whisper in his pious grandmother's ear. And somehow I only rarely made her mad, almost never crossed that invisible line. She knew I respected her. I liked her too, when her all-too-reverent sons were not around to cramp my style and turn her into one of those brightly painted plaster statues over at the Catholic church in Westernport.

I liked her even more when I found out why she was so holy, why she prayed so much, why she was forever asking God to forgive her her terrible sins, and why she always felt impure. There are things I've done, she'd say to my daddy, her voice trailing off. He'd say Miss Maggie, you know you're a good person.

It turns out that Big Mom had two lovers in her long ago youth. One was Daddy Paul, and one was ole Griff Bruce. Now, the rest of what I'm about to tell you was the darkest, deepest family secret in the history of the Coleman family—and we had some good secrets! Strange children showed up at Big Mom's once or twice, with well-dressed colored ladies holding their hands, trying to introduce them to their "grandmother," while my mother was busy trying to call a taxi—"Just as soon as you can possibly get up here ... Yes, that's right ... Coleman ... *Coleman* ... The green house at the top of the hill. Right away!"—all the while using her body and free arm to obstruct from Biggie's line of sight this finely dressed woman with her hair all nicely greased and done, and this little light-brown child, his hair greased down lightly and the part cut properly in an exact straight line on the right side of a not-too-nappy head, dressed in beige shorts, yellow shirt, bow tie, and a jacket to match the shorts, shoes shined, dark brown, with mulatto shoelaces, all of it bought for this monumental encounter. "Lady, I'm sorry," Mama would say, "but you got to *go*," ushering her gently, politely, but firmly out the door and down all those wooden steps that connected Big Mom's swinged porch to the concrete pavement in front of her tenants, the Walkers, below.

Who was that, Mama? I'd ask in feigned innocence, wide-eyed at how much that kid had reminded me of one of Mama's brothers. She had the wrong house, baby, was all that Mama would say. Then I heard Mama call one of her brothers on the telephone after she'd shooed me into the kitchen with Big Mom.

As luck would have it, Big Mom herself had picked as the father of her child a man who turned out not to be the father of her child. It was between Daddy Paul and ole Griff Bruce. Fifty-fifty ain't good odds. Now, according to legend—and this of course I can't verify, since the source was not a Coleman but Daddy's oldest brother, Uncle Lawrence, and how he knew I'll never know—Big Mom went to Griff Bruce and said that she was going to have a baby and that she'd take him if he got rid of his hunting dogs. Griff was a legendary hunter up Williamsport, and if Piedmont was a village, I don't know what Williamsport could have been, since

Piedmont was New York City next to the dusty crossroads with a railroad-track sign that indicated that the municipality of Williamsport existed. (I never saw more than one house in Williamsport, and that was Granny's house, the house where Big Mom was born.)

Well, faced with a choice between those hunting dogs and Big Mom (not to mention Uncle Jim, in the hopper), Griff settled for what he knew and wished Big Mom well in her new life. So she married Daddy Paul. Daddy Paul was dark, with short kinky hair and a straight nose, a certain sense of bearing and of presence. His firstborn child was short, stocky, ruddy in complexion, like the Howards and the Bruces. (Big Mom was a Howard and a Clifford, families who had intermarried with white people and a few genuine Indians for a long time up in those hollows that constitute Williamsport, as well as with each other. If strange things happen at watering holes, as Aristotle said, then things just as strange happen at hollows.) The child had a natural-born capacity to love and hunt and be part of the woods. He also had an uncanny affinity for and knowledge of hunting dogs. And if all that was not enough, he looked like Griff Bruce's clone. Like Griff had spat him out, Uncle Lawrence said.

There Griff was, staring at me in Uncle Jim's face all those years, Daddy said, and I didn't even see it. But once his brother Lawrence told him, it was clear. No denying him.

That was the thing about overhearing genealogical conversations in the colored VFW. Once Pop or Mr. Roebuck Johnson made a pronouncement, the evidence was generally as plain as the nose on your face—or some kid's whose daddy wasn't his daddy and the whole town knew. To tell the truth, the colored people in Piedmont—

men and women, young and old—spent a lot of time talking about sex in general and a fair amount of time detailing the exploits of the midnight warriors who were "sneakin' and creepin'," as we'd say.

It was an epidemic when I was a kid in the fifties—the talk, anyway, including talk about sex with white people, the holiest taboo. How white people couldn't know, I'll never be able to figure out, because everybody colored talked about it all day long. I guess the thing about living in a village at the foot of a mountain is that the world for you becomes, without thinking about it, self-contained. People are of two kinds, really: from the Valley, and from Elsewhere. And there is not a whole lot to keep you occupied. You could play baseball in the summer and basketball year round. You could hunt in the winter, fish in the summer. You could go to the colored Legion, to colored holiday dances.... And you could do the nacky-nacky. For a town with two thousand people, it seemed, there was a whole lot of nacky-nacky, colored and white.

Uncle Joe once told Daddy that he never had *seen* a place where people slept around so much or so openly as they did in Piedmont. *Goddamn*, Daddy would repeat, his voice rising squeakily and irritably high to mimic Uncle Joe's when he is drunk. Goddamn.

As I said, there's just not a lot to do in a small town. And most people there never did mind too much about fornication as a sin, or getting pregnant out of wedlock. Which is not to say that everyone had a healthy, or satisfying, sex life. It is only to say that just about everyone seemed to be sleeping with somebody, or at least that just about everyone spent lots and lots of time talking about sleeping with somebody.

I never saw nothin' at all like Piedmont, Uncle Joe would repeat, shaking his head. They just sleep together all out in the open.

Seeing the twelve Coleman children sitting together (as they did at Christmas dinner Up the Hill at Big Mom's or at the annual Family Reunion in late July) confirmed why Africans in the New World soon came to be called colored people. Their colors ran the full spectrum of brown, like the whole race in miniature, from the richest dark chocolate to the creamiest café au lait.

The Colemans were colored people. In chronological order as in Leviticus, Uncle Jim, or Nemo, was slightly reddish, with a big round head, a heavy build, a short, wide nose, and thin lips. Like all his brothers and sisters, he inherited Big Mom's tiny moles, which develop with age into blotchy skin.

Ed was lighter than Jim, still reddish, though, with a squarer face, high cheekbones, large squinty eyes, closely set. He had a long, straight nose, thin lips, and an even complexion. He was the tallest of the brothers, the wealthiest, and the first to own his own home.

Howard was sleepy-eyed, with a placid face, a long, straight nose, a square jaw, a high forehead, and large eyes. Charles had dark skin, a perfectly round head, wide nose, high cheekbones, lips thicker than the rest of his brothers.

Raymond was a saturated reddish-brown color, and he had a round face with evenly spaced features, his nose short and straight, his eyes smallish. He had the kinkiest hair and was the darkest, which was a source of pain for him for much of my life at least. And the Black Is Beautiful movement didn't seem to help him all that much. To his chagrin, his baby brother, David, had the lightest skin of all and the longest face. David—known as Earkie—was a handsome man, with his aquiline nose and smooth tan skin, his perpetually knitted brows over sad eyes, and his square chin.

Aunt Marguerite and Aunt Loretta had intense eyes with dark

circles around them. Aunt Marguerite's eyes were open, bearing a smart expression. Ham was a caffe latte color, almost orange, and Alvin, the college professor, was a luxurious mahogany. Harry, the "legitimate" preacher (both Nemo and Earkie would get the "call" from God, near retirement time), was a cherrywood brown.

Of all my mama's nine brothers, it was Uncle Earkie with whom I had the most difficult relationship. Not only was he good-looking; he was a sharp dresser and always had a nice new car. A Riviera, say, or an Impala. Not a Pontiac or a Chevy or an Oldsmobile, like everybody else. Earkie had style.

He also had a chip on his shoulder, for reasons that I never really understood . . . until Mama said one day that her father, Daddy Paul, used to beat him, his twelfth child, unmercifully all the time when he was little and accuse him of being someone else's child.

It made me hate my father, Mama would sometimes say. He was a mean man, I guess. Not mean to Mama. But mean to Earkie. And to Uncle Ed too, his first legitimate child. We called him Peck because his initials were P.E.C., for Paul Edwin Coleman. She would tell me about a particular beating that Daddy Paul inflicted upon Uncle Peck, about how horrible it was. Once or twice she'd even cry about it. Years later, when my mother died, we found a diary she had kept in the thirties. On November 28, 1934, when she was eighteen, she had written:

This occurred on the eve of Thanksgiving, November 1934: my father must be the meanest man in this town. After whipping my brother to the skin for stealing coal, until he couldn't beat him any longer, he comes downstairs and slaps my mother in the face as hard as he can because she says to my brother "Don't let him beat you in the face." He doesn't know how to whip a child: He knocks them like dogs. God help him. Then he tells us that we can all go to hell for all he cares. . . . He says if any of us ever turns on him, he will knock us for a row of Sundays. Some day, we are going to do just that.

Earkie still talks about Daddy Paul like he was Solomon, Moses, and the Good Lord Jesus, all rolled into one, just as all his children do except Uncle Harry. I never knew Daddy Paul, since he died at the end of the war, five years before I was born. I only know him through Mama's stories about Earkie. And through that diary entry.

Daddy Paul had standing in the community. "He was a good man," people would say of him, including white people. But his vocation was no more exalted than others'. He worked as a janitor and handyman at the Devon Club, the mill's dry goods store, and raising twelve children on a handyman's salary was a stretch. Never having quite enough—whether food or anything else—was the condition of their childhood, and it marked them all, in different ways.

But Earkie, born almost twenty years after his eldest brother, was marked in yet another way, as he took the beating for an event over which he had no control. Those beatings didn't stop him from becoming a lover, though.

Most people in Piedmont kept their dogs chained to doghouses in their backyards. In the middle of the night, you could hear them barking, as somebody sneakin' and creepin' would steal his way through the darkness into somebody else's bedroom. The chief cause of all that nighttime barking, at least when I was young, was my uncle Earkie, so people said.

Miss Lizzie Johnson's dogs especially would go crazy every night when one of my uncles, baby-sitting at Big Mom's house, would creep down the back stairs and try to sneak past those sleeping dogs to his girlfriend's house. If my uncle had been Jim, with Griff's hunting genes, the boy might have made it. But dogs, after all, have keen ears.

Years later, my friends and I nicknamed him the Sneakin' Deacon. He had joined Uncle Jim's Homemade Baptist Church, declared himself to be both "saved" and a deacon, and kept right on waking Miss Lizzy's hunting dogs every night on his way to visit his friend and keep her company, holding hands and quite possibly talking about the Lord, before he finally got married.

When I was nine or ten, the Coleman Family Reunion was the social event of the season. The only problem was that you had to be a Coleman to be on the list—or else be specially invited. And being invited was one big deal. Even if you were an in-law, you still weren't a Coleman. The Hills, the Stewarts, not to mention the Gateses—these weren't Colemans, at least not according to "the boys," the nine male descendants of Paul Coleman, almost all of whom named one son Paul. (My brother's name is Paul, cousin Greg's middle name is Paul, Uncle Alvin's son is named Paul, even Uncle Jim's younger son is named Paul. I could go on.) That man had power; he perpetuates himself from the grave.

As years went by, I grew more critical, deciding that I was more like the Gateses than the Colemans—a world of difference. Accordingly, I decided that Mama must have been a Howard or a Clifford, because she was totally unlike her sisters and brothers.

The Colemans weren't good storytellers, like my daddy was. They didn't drink, they didn't smoke, and if they weren't especially religious, they were especially self-righteous.

And they had ideas about a woman's place that I knew, even as a child, just were not going to play. One wanted his woman to be home all day long, waiting for him, baking bread and stuff, "so that I smell it when my foot hits the door." We used to wonder if he should try to clone Barbara Eden in *I Dream of Jeannie*, because that's about what he'd need.

They didn't exactly practice sexual equality in that family. Up at Big Mom's on Christmas, the men would be seated first, at the formal dining table with the extra leaves, while the women served them. They even served the *boys* first, before they returned to the kitchen to eat their own supper, with Big Mom. Then they'd clear the tables and wash up. The men retired to the living room, to watch football and chew on the facts of life, sipping iced tea diluted with fast-melting but regularly replenished cubes of ice, a wedge of lemon hooked on the glass's side.

Nobody thought anything about this arrangement until I brought my wife, Sharon, to dinner up there in 1973. When she sat down at the table with the men, you could have heard a pin drop. But the women served her, too, while the Coleman boys bumbled around, trying to figure out what to say, "skinning 'em back," as Pop says when black people Tom up to white people, saying hee-hee-hee a lot.

That was our last Christmas dinner Up the Hill at Big Mom's.

Colemans didn't hang out with other colored people very much. Classed off, as the tradition says. You'd never find a Coleman at the colored VFW. Come to that, I never remember seeing one down at

Mr. Comby's barbershop, except for Uncle Joe, Aunt Marguerite's husband, who is a Hill and is half white. He and my father would hang out on the edges of Coleman family gatherings, woofing on events and persons in a barely audible stage whisper, like a two-person Greek chorus. "Looks like the mourners' pew at a country funeral," I heard one of them say to the other at a reunion. And as soon as I looked over at "the boys," sitting somberly in a row at the picnic table, I busted out laughing. These guys could rain on any parade when they got together. It was a major preoccupation of theirs, sitting around rattling ice in tall plastic cups of iced tea, like blackbirds in a rhythm band, Daddy would say. They had a weighty sense of family and tradition. Almost all of them became born-again Christians near the end, like Big Mom's brother, Uncle Boke, just before he went crazy.

Big Mom took Boke's death kind of hard. He was her younger brother. Otis Howard his proper name was, rhiney-colored leader of the Colored Prayer Band, head deacon and agent of the Holy Ghost, keeping watch for the Return of the Lord Himself. *Jee-zuhs.*

We had been playing on the playground, toward the middle of Erin Street. Aunt Ruth sold lemonade to the kids, and a water fountain did for our thirst what her lemonade couldn't do. The playground had monkey bars and a sliding board that must have been twenty feet tall, a basketball hoop and a baseball field and plenty of places to bike. I was on the monkey bars, sitting up there just swinging my legs, with a straight-ahead view of Uncle Boke's front door. He began running out with his hands in the air, imploring the Lord to take him now. He'd run outside to the middle of the road, shout and pray, and then he'd run back in. Three hours later, the message changed: The world was ending that day.

We thought it was funny, of course, and embarrassing. But as his behavior continued, it became scary, then sad. By nightfall, they had come to get him, hauling him off to Lakin, the colored insane asylum. Shoot me first, was all Daddy said, except to add that Boke had always been crazy, citing the night he had waited six hours in the rain at the bus stop at the bottom of Big Mom's hill for a phantom woman to return on a phantom bus. You see, one day Boke announced that Theresa Price, a black woman who was much younger than he was, was coming on the bus to meet him at the bus stop at the bottom of the hill in Piedmont. She never came; she was never going to. He had fantasized it all, in an earlier phase of his madness. He just stood there for hours in the rain, meeting all the buses. Had his good umbrella there too, Daddy pointed out, so she wouldn't be getting wet. Wonder what would have happened, he sometimes asks, if she actually showed up on that bus?

The thing about them niggers, Daddy says about his in-laws with grudging admiration, was that they wanted to be self-sufficient. They'd drive fifty miles to save fifty cents, but they were ambitious and knew how to do things. Daddy meant that they were good with their hands. Carpentry, masonry, gardening, hunting, fishing. Just fixing things in general. If you can hammer it or oil it up, dem coons can do it.

The nine Coleman boys, with birth dates ranging from 1915 to 1933, were the last generation in our family conceived, born, and bred under segregation. Cradle-to-grave segregation. They were poor but talented and motivated. And they had to learn to stitch with the odds and ends left over from the bolts of whole cloth sitting on top of the tailor's table. Piecework. Colored piecework. Born barely working class—clawing and scraping your way out of starvation class, Daddy says—they carved out a dark-chocolate world, a world as nurturing as the loamy soil in Nemo's garden down at the bottom of Rat Tail Road. The tangle of family ties served as the netting that covered the garden's yield, setting it off from the chaos of flora that nature threw up in its undifferentiated madness of creation. That netting kept out predators, like birds and insects, who would wreak havoc on the order that weeks and months of after-hours labor had created. They would mouth the white man's commands in the day, to paraphrase Hurston, and enact their own legislation and jurisprudence in their sepia world at night.

The soul of that world was colored. Its inhabitants went to colored schools, they went to colored churches, they lived in colored neighborhoods, they ate colored food, they listened to colored music, and when all that fat and grease finally closed down their arteries or made their hearts explode, they slept in colored cemeteries, escorted there by colored preachers: old black-suited Southern preachers, with shiny black foreheads and an insatiable desire for fried chicken, men for whom preaching is a personal call from God, a direct line on His celestial cellular phone. They dated colored, married colored, divorced and cheated on colored. And when they could, they taught at colored colleges, preached to colored congregations, trimmed colored hair on nappy heads, and, after the fifties, even fought to keep alive the tradition of the segregated all-colored schools. They feared that world where so much humiliation had lain in wait, ambushing them blindsided, unawares. And they hated that which made them fear. That is, I think, why they hated some of us, the first generation of integrated wannabes, recognizing us as the real threat to the ordered universe they had constructed with such painstaking care for such a long time. It was like hoeing an acre of drought-stricken land with a wooden stick, Uncle Jim told me one day, out in the fishing boat, referring to their efforts to purchase the houses where they now lived.

Take the family reunions. The Coleman Family Reunion was inaugurated in 1949, the year before I was born. Nemo would ask permission of Mr. Baines or Mr. Bonner to use an acre of his farm, one that bordered Patterson's Creek or the South Branch of the Potomac. And we'd all gather there on the last Sunday in July, lounging on blankets that covered any overlooked cow pies, feasting off makeshift dining tables assembled for the occasion out of no. 2 pine two-by-fours. We'd play softball and badminton all day, swimming in between to cool ourselves off or to digest the feast of wonders that "the women" had prepared—from Aunt Marguerite's potato salad and Aunt Dot's fried chicken to Aunt Mary Jane's homemade cranberry sauce and Dorothy Ann's German chocolate cake, all washed down with Nemo's famous homemade root beer. Raymond took great pride in slicing the watermelon at the end of the day, the very last thing you did before cleaning up and stowing everything away in the trunks of the cars, to start the long journey back home to Piedmont, a world distant and all of ten or fifteen miles away.

Eventually they'd persuaded a real estate agent to part with an acre in a new development on the South Branch, then built the Coleman summer house, brick by brick, nail by nail, with their own hands, getting Teddy Twyman, the colored electrician up at the paper mill, to help with the wiring. In a hundred-acre field of trailers and Winnebagos, the Coleman boys had constructed a five-room house, complete with fireplace and picture window, a shower and a screened-in porch and, a hundred feet away, a pavilion covering a table large enough to seat us all. And they did this before any of the rednecks who would be our neighbors could murmur any protest or raise even the barest hum of a fuss. Soon, in imitation, they started trying to turn their trailers into homes, structures with porches and cement foundations, just to keep up with the colored. Too late to burn the house down. Besides, hill folk generally didn't do that kind of thing. As long as there was only one colored in the field, things would be all right. Planted sod, too, and kept it neat. Showplace, the hill folk called it. A colored showplace.

Jarvis Q. DeBerry

Roy Lee DeBerry

My grandfather was a tree. Not so tall, but sturdy, solid enough for generations to lean on him.

His name was Roy Lee DeBerry, and his dark skin glowed like a polished wood floor. He talked about God as if the two of them were fishing buddies. As Sunday School Superintendent and church deacon, he offered up prayers that sounded cocky, as if he knew—just knew!—that of all the requests that landed on God's desk, his would get top priority.

He was a tree. His branches shielded, shaded, and sheltered his family from harm. He used to sit on one of the folding chairs next to the other deacons, and when it was his turn to lead a song, he'd consistently choose "Shine On Me." You shouldn't interpret that as selfishness, though. He needed that light to survive. He needed that light so his family could thrive.

Hours before his funeral, I went to the funeral home alone, needing to have my own private moment with him. You know the strangest thing about seeing him in his coffin? His nose. DeBerrys have big noses: fleshy inverted funnels. This nose was small. Like someone taking a file to a wood carving, my grandfather's nose now had angles! How do I mourn if the body that is isn't the body that was?

During the final year of Big Daddy's life, the last in a series of strokes pulled his eyes open wide as a doe's. He could no longer speak, and his right leg became permanently bent at the knee. Imagine pulling your legs in close to let a late churchgoer squeeze in and take the seat next to you. That's how it was, except it was only his right leg. No one could pull it straight again—not his doctors, not any of his six sons.

Standing over his coffin, I remembered Bob, a family friend who likes to laugh at the expense of others, telling stories about working for a Detroit funeral home. He said his crew would sometimes find the deceased bent into the shape of a favorite chair, or, less romantically, sitting cold, dead, and exposed on the toilet. And then he said, as if it were just the funniest thing, that the only way to stretch such a body out is to break a few of its bones.

My grandfather died in a hospital bed in Tupelo, Mississippi, but he died with his right leg bent into a "V." I looked down at his strange face with its nasal bone jutting out and I heard his leg snap like a twig.

My Uncle Ronald is the baby of the family, the youngest of eleven children. He talks the most and (not coincidentally) he is the most ignored. One time, though, he and his siblings stood on the porch swapping "worst whuppin'" stories. My grandfather was there, sitting in his chair, looking out at the road and pretending like he wasn't listening. Uncle Ronald entered the contest with his account of the day he played hooky and then felt the rod of Roy Lee DeBerry. Skipping school was foolish enough. But my uncle made the unbelievably brazen move of returning home in the middle of the day.

The nosy neighbor next door saw him as he sneaked into the

house, and she immediately picked up the phone and called the office building where my grandfather worked as a janitor. Within minutes, the man was home. But even though he searched the front room, the bedrooms, the closets, the bathroom, and the kitchen, he didn't find his son. Ronald had climbed into the attic when he heard the front door open. He stayed there and waited for the screen door slam that would signal his father's departure. After he heard it, he waited a few thundering heartbeats, climbed down from the attic, and sprinted to the corner store where the owner would give him a quarter for sweeping the floor.

He was immersed in his work when he happened to look up and take in a sight that twenty-five years later he would remember in all of its frightening detail: Roy Lee DeBerry, belt raised over his head, charging at him.

The man seemed to have no shame. He began swinging the belt inside the store, used it to herd his stray sheep home, and once inside the house he really let it whistle. Not only was he angry that he had to take off from work, but he was even more upset that his boy was squandering his chance at an education.

When he was satisfied that he'd done enough, he dragged his son back to school and presented him to W. H. "Chick" Henderson, a paddling principal who folks said could show Hank Aaron something about a sweet swing. When he comforted Roy Lee with the promise that he'd fix the truant right there in his office, the father paused, then shook his head in disapproval.

"Naw, tell you what you do, Chick. Take him in front of his class. Get him there. That'll learn him."

Years later, the son remembered this out loud and my grandfather began chuckling at the memory. And that's when Uncle Ronald said something that got everybody's attention: "Yeah, when we were growing up, wasn't but one man at this house." He made eye contact with each of his five older brothers. The oldest was more than sixty years old. Uncle Ronald looked back at the man who raised them all, took a gulp of beer, and said, "Shoot, ain't but one man here now."

◀

I feel like a boy. On this day, the day of Big Daddy's funeral, I wonder if this isn't what every male in my family is feeling: small, impotent, not quite ready to be called a man.

None of us knows the proper way to mourn. The women seem to know instinctively. They are inside, patting sobs out of one another's backs, each within hugging distance of another.

We are outside, spread out, each safe from the contagion of the other's sorrow. Conery, my cousin, sucks a Newport. Uncle James, a Benson & Hedges. Some fold their arms and kick at the loose gravel at the edge of the driveway.

I am at the side of the house leaning against the wall and looking down at the water hose my cousins and I used to bring to our lips between kickball games. Tears leak from my eyes: enough tears, I hope, that I can keep my composure when I arrive at church and read the tribute I've written for Big Daddy.

The night Mama told me Big Daddy was dead, I told her I would write a tribute to read at his funeral. I was talking to her because my daddy was frustrating me. His daddy's body wasn't even cold yet and he was talking to me about how he had to be a man, how he had to just (sigh) keep on going, 'cause that's what Big

Daddy taught his boys to do: be strong. He was explaining this strange emotional rigidity of his as reasonableness, as manhood.

So what did that make me? I was hyperventilating.

So I was talking to my mother. She asked if I thought I could handle reading a tribute and, in answering her, I tried my best to sound like my father, whom I wanted to be like even as I was silently screaming at him. I answered my mother with three words: "I have to."

There's been at least one at every funeral I've attended: the person who stands and—under the pretense of comforting—begins criticizing those who cry. Using clichés about this and that side of Jordan, she explains that the deceased is in a sorrow-free place and that we on this side would be selfish to wish him back here.

I don't remember now who played that role at my grandfather's funeral, but for the first time I understand.

The person in that coffin is not my Big Daddy. My Big Daddy was strong and powerfully built, not the shell of a man resting on top of that white satin. My Big Daddy had a nose that weighted down his face like an anchor.

I understand, finally. I laugh at all the funny stories told about him. Punch lines don't really punch at funerals, but I laugh anyway. I smile when Eddie Lee Smith, Jr., the man still serving as Holly Springs' first black mayor, tells the congregation that he has just returned from Jackson, that he has seen the Mississippi Sovereignty Commission's recently-opened records on "dangerous" black folks, black folks who were visible and vocal in the push for equal protection under the law. Roy Lee DeBerry's name was listed among the troublemakers.

My cousins—my fellow pallbearers—are crying into their palms, their heads close to their knees; but I feel good. My eyes are dry, and I keep my head held high as if I have grasped some emotional truth they have not. I stand and read the audience a card I had mailed to Big Daddy when I heard a man in St. Louis sing a spiritless rendition of "Shine on Me." In the letter I tell him how much the song had made me miss him; to the congregation I analyze his love for the hymn.

Big Daddy was photosynthetic. He absorbed God's light. We, in turn, breathed in Big Daddy's love.

How can his coffin be so heavy? My grandfather weighed ninety pounds when he died, yet as we lift him out of the hearse, I feel a tugging, separating pain in my elbow and in my shoulder.

Big Daddy never got used to being carried. He told me as much, the day I joined him on the porch as he sat waving at the cars going past on Boundary Street. I told him I had just bumped into a woman who, when she found out my last name, asked if I was related to Roy Lee DeBerry. She was a nurse who had taken care of him after his first stroke, and she told me—with a smile—that he got on her nerves more than any other patient she'd ever had. She said she'd never met anybody so stubborn, so determined not to be helped.

Big Daddy shook his head and laughed. He said that nurse was tough, that she had gotten on his nerves, too. "I just ain't never had to depend on nobody before," he said. He watched a few cars pass.

Then, as if he really didn't mean to speak this truth out loud, whispered, "Folks depended on me."

He bit his bottom lip; I turned away when I saw the tear forming in the corner of his eye. We didn't say anything else. We watched the cars go down Boundary Street. We lifted our arms and waved.

The next time I saw my grandfather, he was sitting at the edge of a recliner with his right leg bent at the knee. He was staring at me with wide eyes that never seemed to blink. He did not know who I was; or maybe he did, and had no way to prove it.

I just ain't never had to depend on nobody before.

Well, he has to depend on us, his grandsons, to get him to his grave, and even now he isn't cooperating. The year before, my 250-pound cousin Connel dropped dead, and his coffin was amazingly light.

I didn't expect to have so much trouble carrying my grand-father to his grave, and yet I am stumbling, trying to put one polished shoe in front of the other, wondering if my other cousins are thinking what I am: Big Daddy is the heaviest load we've ever had to carry.

I blame my grandmother. Big Mama had already come close to making me cry earlier, back at the house before the procession left for the church. She had sat in her chair wearing her black suit and gray gloves, and sighing. No words, no tears; just a sigh.

I imagined that she was thinking of her wedding. Willie Mae McEwen was an eighteen-year-old bride, walking down the aisle with the short, pretty-talking boy who had wooed her on the school ground, the boy she had known most of her life. He left her an eighty-year-old widow.

Is it possible for any human being to remember the details of a life lived sixty-two years ago?

Big Mama had come close to making me cry when I was standing behind her at her house, patting her back. Now I am standing next to her, staring down at the rectangle that is swallowing my grandfather. She does not cry. She fingers the rose handed to her by the undertaker, and tosses it onto her husband's casket.

"Well," she says, "I ain't got nobody to help me now. You gone."

Something inside me snaps.

I feel my lungs gather a gulp of air.

A tree stands in the distance, and I start walking toward it.

Fred D'Aguiar

A Son in Shadow

I know nothing about how they meet. She is a schoolgirl. He is at work, probably a government clerk in a building near her school. At the hour when school and office are out for lunch their lives intersect at sandwich counters, soft-drink stands, traffic lights, market squares. Their eyes meet or their bodies collide at one of these food queues. He says something suggestive, complimentary. She suppresses a smile or traps one beneath her hands. He takes this as encouragement (as if any reaction of hers would have been read as anything else) and keeps on talking and following her and probably misses lunch that day. All the while she walks and eats and drinks and soaks up his praise, his sweet body-talk, his erotic chatter and sexy pitter-patter, his idle boasts and ample toasts to his life, his dreams about their future, the world their oyster together.

Am I going too fast on my father's behalf? Should there have been an immediate and cutting rebuttal from her and several days before another meeting? Does he leave work early to catch her at the end of the schoolday and follow her home just to see where she lives and to extend the boundaries of their courtship? Throwing it from day to night, from school to home, from childhood play to serious adult intent? Georgetown's two-lane streets with trenches on either side mean a mostly single-file walk, she in front probably looking over her shoulder when he says something worthy of a glance, or a cut-eye look if his suggestions about her body or what he will do with it if given half a chance exceed the decorum of the day—which is what, in mid-fifties Guyana? From my grandmother it's "Don't talk to a man unless you think you're a big woman. Man will bring you trouble. Man want just one thing from you. Don't listen to he. Don't get ruined for he. A young lady must cork her ears and keep her eye straight in front of she when these men start to flock around. The gentleman among them will find his way to her front door. The gentleman will make contact with the parents first. Woo them first before muttering one thing to the young lady. Man who go directly to young ladies only want to ruin them. Don't want to make them into respectable young women—just whores. Mark my words." My grandfather simply thinks that his little girl is not ready for the attentions of any man, that none of them is good enough for his little girl, and so the man who comes to his front door had better have a good pretext for disturbing his reverie. He had better know something about merchant seamen and the character of the sea, and about silence—how to keep it so that it signifies authority and dignity, so when you speak you are heard and your words, every one of them, are rivets. That man would have to be a genius to get past my grandfather, a genius or a gentleman. And since my father is neither, it's out of the question that he'll even use the front door of worship. His route will have to be the yard and the street of ruination.

So he stands in full view of her house at dusk. It takes a few nights before her parents realize he is there for their daughter. Then one day her father comes out and tells him to take his dog behavior to someone else's front door, and the young man quickly turns on his heel and walks aways. Another time her mother opens the upstairs window and curses him, and he laughs and saunters off as if her words were a broom gently ushering him out of her yard. But he returns the next night and the next, and the daughter can't believe his determination. She is embarrassed that her body has been a magnet for trouble, that she is the cause of the uproar, then angry with him for his keen regard of her at the expense of her dignity, not to mention his. Neighbors tease her about him. They take pity on the boy, offer him drinks, some ice-cold maubey, a bit to eat, a dhal-pouri, all of which he declines at first, then dutifully accepts. One neighbor even offers him a chair, and on one night of pestilential showers an umbrella, since he does not budge from his spot while all around him people dash for shelter, abandoning a night of liming (loitering) and gaffing (talking) to the persistence and chatter of the rain. Not my father. He stands his ground, with only the back of his right hand up to his brow to shelter his eyes zeroed in on her house. She steals a glance at him after days of seeming to ignore the idea of him, though his presence burns brightly inside her heart. She can't believe his vigilance is for her. She stops to stare in the mirror and for the first time sees her full lips, long straight nose, shoulder-length brunette hair, and dark green eyes with their slight oval shape. Her high cheekbones. Her ears close to her skull. She runs her fingers lightly over these places as if to touch is to believe. Her lips tingle. Her hair shines. Her eyes smile. And she knows from this young man's perseverance that she is beautiful, desirable. She abandons herself to chores, and suppresses a smile and a song. She walks past windows as much as possible to feed the young man's hungry eyes with a morsel of that which he has venerated to the point of indignity. She rewards his eyes by doing unnecessary half-turns at the upstairs window. A flash of clavicle, a hand slowly putting her hair off her face and setting it down behind her ears, and then a smile, a demure glance, her head inclined a little, her eyes raised, her eyelids batted a few times—she performs for him, though she feels silly and self-conscious. What else is there for a girl to do? Things befitting a lady that she picked up from the cinema. Not the sauciness of a tramp.

Her mother pulls her by one of those beautiful closed-skulled ears from the window and curses her, as if she were a ten-cent whore, then throws open the window and hurtles a long list of insults at this tall, silent, rude, good-for-nothing streak of impertinence darkening her street. The father folds his paper and gets up, but by the time he gets to the window the young man is gone.

My mother cries into the basin of dishes. She rubs a saucer so hard that it comes apart in her hands. She is lucky not to cut herself. She will have to answer to her mother for that breakage. In the past it meant at least a few slaps and many minutes of curses for bringing only trouble into her mother's house. Tonight her mother is even angrier. Her father has turned his fury against her for rearing a daughter who is a fool for men. Her mother finds her in the kitchen holding the two pieces of the saucer together and then apart—as if her dread and sheer desire for reparation would magically weld them whole. Her tears fall like drops of solder on that divided saucer. Her mother grabs her hands and strikes her and curses her into her face so that my mother might as well be standing over a steaming, spluttering pot on the stove. She drops the two pieces of saucer and they become six pieces. Her mother looks down and strides over the mess with threats about what will happen if her feet find a splinter. She cries but finds every piece, and to be sure to get the splinters too she runs her palms along the floor, this way and that, and with her nails she prizes out whatever her hand picks up. She cries herself to sleep.

The next night he is back at his station, and her mother and father, their voices, their words, their blows, sound a little farther off, fall a little lighter. His presence, the barefaced courage of it, becomes a suit of armor for her to don against her mother's and father's attacks. She flies through her chores. She manages under her mother's watchful eye to show both sides of her clavicle, even a little of the definition down the middle of her chest—that small trench her inflated chest digs, which catches the light and takes the breath away, that line drawn from the throat to the uppermost rib exuding warmth and tension, drawing the eyes twenty-five yards away with its radiance in the half-light of dusk, promising more than it can possibly contain, than the eye can hold, and triggering a normal heart into palpitations, a normal breath into shallowness and rapidity.

"Miss Isiah, howdy! How come you house so clean on the west side and not so clean on the east? It lopsided! Dirt have a preference in your house? Or is that saga boy hanging around the west side of your house a dirt repellent?" The gossip must have been rampant in the surrounding yards, yards seemingly designed deliberately so people could see into one another's homes and catch anything spilling out of them—quarrels, courtships, cooking pots, music—and sometimes a clash of houses, a reaction against the claustrophobia of the yard, but not enough yards, not enough room to procure a necessary privacy in order to maintain a badly sought-after dignity— clean, well-dressed, head high in the air on Sundays—impossible if the night before there is a fight and everyone hears you beg not to be hit anymore, or else such a stream of obscenities gushes from your mouth that the sealed red lips of Sunday morning just don't cut it.

My father maintains his vigil. Granny threatens to save the contents of her chamber pot from the night before and empty it on his head. Could she have thrown it from her living room window to his shaded spot by the street? Luckily, she never tries. She may well be telling him that he doesn't deserve even that amount of attention. If there is any creature lower than a gutter rat—one too low to merit even her worst display of disdain—then he is it. How does my father take that? As a qualification he can do without? How much of that kind of water is he able to let run off his back? Poor man. He has to be in love. He has to be wearing his own suit of armor. Lashed to his mast like Odysseus, he hears the most taunting, terrible things, but what saves him, what restores him, is the ropes, the armor of his love for my mother. Others without this charm would have withered away, but my father smiles and shrugs at the barrage of looks, insults, gestures, silence, loneliness.

Watch his body there under that breadfruit or sapodilla tree; the shine of his status as sentry and his conviction are twin headlights that blind her parents. They redouble their efforts to get rid of his particular glare, then are divided by the sense of his inevitability in their daughter's life. My grandmother stops shouting at him while my grandfather still raises his cane and causes the young man to walk away briskly. My grandmother then opens the windows on the west side, ostensibly to let in the sea breeze but really to exhibit in all those window frames a new and friendly demeanor. My grandfather shouts at her that he can smell the rank intent of that black boy, rotten as a fish market, blowing into his living room and spoiling his thoughts.

But the windows stay open. And my mother at them. With the love Morse of her clavicles and her cleavage as she grows bolder. Smiling, then waving. And no hand in sight to box her or grip her by the ear and draw her away from there. Until one night she boldly leaves the house and goes to him and they talk for five minutes rapidly, as if words are about to run out in the Southern Hemisphere.

◢

My father's parents wonder what has become of their Gordon.

"The boy only intend to visit town."

"Town swallow him up."

"No, one woman turn he head, stick it in a butter churn and swill it."

"He lost to us now."

"True."

They say this to each other but hardly speak to him except to make pronouncements on the size of foreign lands.

"Guyana small?"

"What's the boy talking about?"

"Why, England and Scotland combined are the size of Guyana."

"How much room does a man need?"

"That woman take he common sense in a mortar and pound it with a pestle."

The two voices are one voice.

Opportunity is here now. The English are letting go of the reins, a whole new land is about to be fashioned. And he is planning to leave! What kind of woman has done this to our boy? The boy is lost. Talking to him is like harnessing a stubborn donkey. This isn't love but voodoo, obeah, juju, some concoction in a drink, some spell thrown in his locus. A little salt over the shoulder, an iodine shower, a rabbit foot on a string, a duck's bill or snake head dried and deposited into the left trouser pocket, a precious stone, lapis lazuli, amethyst, or anything on the middle finger, a good old reliable crucifix around the neck, made of silver, not gold, and at least one ounce in weight and two inches in diameter. A psalm in papyrus folded in a shirt pocket next to the heart. A blessing from a priest, a breathing of nothing but incense with a towel over the head. A bout of fasting, one night without sleep, a dreamless night, and a dreamless, sleepless, youngest son restored to them. He wants to stay around the house, he shows them why he loves his mummy and poppy and the bounteous land. There is no plan to flee. There is no city woman with his heart in her hand. And his brain is not ablaze in his pants. His head is not an empty, airless room.

They have one cardboard suitcase each, apart from her purse and his envelope tied with a string that contains their passports and tickets, birth certificates, and, for him, a document that he is indeed a clerk with X amount of experience at such-and-such a government office, signed "supervisor"—a worthless piece of shit, of course, in the eyes of any British employer. But for the time being, these little things are emblematic of the towering, staggering optimism that propels them out of Georgetown, Guyana, over the sea to London, England.

So what do they do? My mother is a shy woman. My father, in the two photos I've seen of him, is equally reserved. Not liable to experimentation. The big risk has been taken—that of leaving everything they know for all that is alien to them. My mother knows next to nothing about sex, except perhaps a bit about kissing. My father may have experimented a little, as boys tend to do, but he too, when faced with the female body, confronts unfamiliar territory. Each burns for the other, enough to pull up roots and take off into the unknown. Yet I want to believe that they improvise around the idea of her purity and respect it until their marriage night. That they keep intact some of the moral system they come from even as they dismantle and ignore every other stricture placed on them by Guyanese society: honor your father and mother; fear a just and loving God; pledge allegiance to the flag; lust is the devil's oxygen. All that circles in their veins.

Over the twelve days at sea they examine what they have left and what they are heading toward. At sea they are in between lives: one life is over but the other has not yet begun. The talking they do on that ship, without any duties to perform at all! My mother tells how her father, despite his routine as a merchant seaman, finds time to memorize whole poems by the Victorians: Tennyson, Longfellow, Browning, Jean Ingelow, Arnold, and Hopkins. The sea is his workplace, yet he makes time to do this marvelous thing. She tells how when he comes back to land he gathers them all in the living room and performs "The Charge of the Light Brigade" or "Maud" or "My Last Duchess" or "Fra Lippo Lippi" or "The High Tide on the Coast of Lincolnshire" or "Dover Beach" or "The Kingfisher" or "The Wreck of the *Deutschland.*" He recites these poems to his Creole-thinking children, who sit there and marvel at the English they are hearing, not that of the policeman or the teacher or the priest, but even more difficult to decipher, full of twists and impossible turns that throw you off the bicycle of your Creole reasoning into the sand. If any of them interrupts my grandfather, he stops in midflow, tells them off in Creole, and resumes his poem where he left off. When particularly miffed by the disturbance, he starts the poem from the beginning again. Does my grandfather recite these verses before or after he gets drunk, swears at the top of his voice, and chases my grandmother around the house with his broad leather belt?

But when my parents are out to sea, they have only the King James Bible in their possession. What they plan and rehearse is every aspect of their new life.

"Children. I want children."

"Me too. Plenty of them."

"I can work between births."

"Yes, both of us. Until we have enough money for a house. Then you can stay home with the kids."

"A nanny. Someone to watch the kids while we work. What kind of house?"

"Three bedrooms. A garden at the front, small, and back, large. A car—a Morris Minor. With all that room in the back for the children and real indicators and a wood finish." Neither has a notebook or dreamed of keeping one. They do not write their thoughts, they utter them. If something is committed to memory, there has to be a quotidian reason for it, apart from bits of the Bible and a few calypsos. My grandfather's labor of love, his settling down with a copy of Palgrave's *Golden Treasury* and memorizing lines that bear no practical relationship to his life, must seem bizarre to his children. Yet by doing so he demonstrates his love of words, their music, the sense of their sound, their approximation to the heartbeat and breath, their holding out of an alternative world to the one surrounding him, their confirmation of a past and another's life and thoughts, their luxury of composition, deliberation, their balancing and rebalancing of a skewered life. I imagine my mother benefits from this exposure in some oblique way—that the Victorians stick to her mental makeup whether she cares for them or not, that a little of them comes off on me in the wash of my gestation in her.

There is an old black-and-white photo (isn't there always?) and fragments of stories about his comings and goings, his carryings-on, as the West Indian speak goes, his mischief. "Look pan that smooth face, them two big, dark eye them, don't they win trust quick-time? Is hard to tie the man with them eye in him head to any woman and she pickney them. He face clean-shaven like he never shave. He curly black hair, dougla-look, but trim neat-neat. The man got topside." His hair, thick and wavy because of the "dougla" mix of East Indian and black, exaggerates an already high forehead. Automatically we credit such an appearance, in the Caribbean and elsewhere, with intelligence—"topside." And a European nose, not broad, with a high bridge (good breeding, though the nostrils flare a bit—sign of a quick temper!). And lips that invite kisses. "They full-full and pout like a kiss with the sound of a kiss way behind, long after that kiss come and gone." He is six feet tall and thin but not skinny, that brand of thin that women refer to as elegant, since the result is long fingers and economic gestures. Notice I say economic and not cheap. A man of few words. A watcher. "But when he relax in company he know and trust, then he the center of wit and idle philosophizing. He shoot back a few rums, neat no chaser, with anyone, and hold his own with men more inclined to gin and tonic. He know when to mind he p's and q's and when to gaff in the most lewd Georgetown rumshop talk with the boys. What chance a sixteen-year-old closeted lady got against such a man, I ask you?"

But most of the puzzle is missing. So I start to draw links from one fragment to the next. He begins to belong—fleetingly, at first— in my life. As a man in poor light seen crossing a road mercifully free of traffic, its tarmacadam steamy with a recent downpour. As a tall, lank body glimpsed ducking under the awning of a shopfront and disappearing inside and never emerging, no matter how long I wait across the street, watching the door with its reflecting plate glass and listening for the little jingle of the bell that announces the arrival and departure of customers.

Or I cross Blackheath Hill entranced by the urgent belief that my father is in one of the cars speeding up and down it. Blackheath Hill curves a little with a steep gradient—less than one in six in places. It's more of a ski slope than a hill. Cars and trucks, motorbikes and cyclists all come down the road as if in a race for a finish line. Going up it is no different. Vehicles race to the top as if with the fear that their engines might cut off and they will slide back down. I want to be seen by my father. I have to be close to his car so that he does not miss me. I measure the traffic and watch myself get halfway, then, after a pause to allow a couple of cars to pass on their way up, a brisk walk, if I time it right, to allow the rest of the traffic to catch up with me, to see the kid who seems to be in no particular hurry to get out of their way looking at them. I step onto the sidewalk and cherish the breeze of the nearest vehicle at my back—Father, this is your son you have just missed. Isn't he big? Pull over and call his name. Take him in your arms. Admonish him. Remind him that cars can kill and his little body would not survive a hit at these high speeds. Tell him to look for his father under less dangerous circumstances.

I am searching the only way I know how, by rumination, contemplation, conjecture, supposition. I try to fill the gaps, try to piece together the father I never knew. I imagine everything where there is little or nothing to go on. And yet, in going back, in raking up bits and pieces of a shattered and erased existence, I know that I am courting rejection from a source hitherto silent and beyond me. I am conjuring up a father safely out of reach and taking the risk that the lips I help to move, the lungs I force to breathe, will simply say "No." No to everything I ask of them, even the merest crumb of recognition.

"Father." The noun rings hollowly when I say it, my head is empty of any meaning the word might have. I shout it in a dark cave, but none of the expected bats come flapping out. Just weaker and weaker divisions of my call. "Father." It is my incantation to bring him back from the grave to the responsibility of his name. But how, when I only know his wife, my mother, and her sudden, moody silence whenever he crops up in conversation?

You ever have anyone sweet-talk you? Fill your ears with their kind of wax, rub that wax with their tongue all over your body with more promises than the promised land itself contains, fill your head with their sweet drone, their buzz that shuts out your parents, friends, your own mind from its own house? That's your father, the bumblebee, paying attention to me.

My sixteenth birthday was a month behind. He was nearly twenty. A big man in my eyes. What did he want with me? A smooth tongue in my ears. Mostly, though, he watched me, my house, my backside when he followed me home from school. His eyes gleamed in the early evening, the whites of his eyes. He stood so still by the side of the road outside my house that he might have been a lamppost, planted there, shining just for me.

My father cursed him, my mother joined in, my sisters laughed at his silence, his stillness. They all said he had to be the most stupid man in Georgetown, a dunce, a bat in need of a perch, out in the sun too long, sun fry his brain, cat take his tongue, his head empty like a calabash, his tongue cut out, he look like a beggar. They felt sorry for him standing there like a paling, his face a yard long, his tongue a slab of useless plywood in his mouth. "Look what Ingrid gone and bring to the house, shame, dumbness, blackness follow she here to we house to paint shame all over it and us. Go away, black boy, take your dumb misery somewhere else, crawl back to your pen in the country, leave we sister alone, she got more beauty than sense to listen to a fool like you, to let you follow her, to encourage you by not cursing the day you was born and the two people who got together to born you and your people and the whole sorry village you crawl out of to come and plant yourself here in front of we house on William Street, a decent street, in Kitty, in we capital."

I should have thanked my sisters; instead I begged them to leave him alone. Ignore him and he'll go away. My father left the house to get hold of the boy by the scruff of his neck and boot his backside out of Kitty, but he ran off when my father appeared in the door frame. With the light of the house behind him and casting a long, dark shadow, he must have looked twice his size and in no mood to bargain. Your father sprinted away, melting into the darkness. I watched for his return by checking that the windows I'd bolted earlier really were bolted, convincing myself that I had overlooked one of them, using my hands to feel the latch as I searched the street for him. But he was gone for the night. My knight. Shining eyes for armor.

My mother cursed him from the living room window, flung it open and pointed at him and with her tongue reduced him to a pile of rubble and scattered that rubble over a wide area, then picked her way through the strewn wreckage to make sure her destruction was complete: "Country boy, what you want with my daughter? What make you think you man enough for her? What you got between your legs that give you the right to plant yourself in front of my house? What kind of blight you is? You fungus!"

As she cursed him and he retreated from the house sheepishly, she watched her husband for approval. These were mild curses for her, dutiful curses, a warm-up. When she really got going, her face reddened and her left arm carved up the air in front of her as if it were the meat of her opponent being dissected into bite-size bits. That's how I knew she was searching for a way to help me but hadn't yet found it. Not as long as my father was at home. Soon he would be at sea, away for weeks, and things would be different.

That is, if my onlooker, my remote watcher, my far-off admirer wasn't scared off forever. And what if he was? Then he didn't deserve me in the first place. If he couldn't take a few curses, he wasn't good for anything. If I wasn't worth taking a few curses for... well, I didn't want a man who didn't think I was worth taking a few curses for! I loved him for coming back night after night when all he got from me was a glance at the window.

Sometimes less than a glance. Just me passing across the window frame as I dashed from chore to chore under four baleful eyes.

It seemed like he was saving all his breath and words for when he could be alone with me. Then he turned on the bumblebee of himself and I was the hapless flower of his attentions. He told me about my skin that it was silk, that all the colors of the rainbow put together still didn't come close to my beautiful skin. That my face, my eyes, my mouth, my nose, the tip of my nose, my ears, my fingertips, each was a precious jewel, precious stone. He likened the rest of me to things I had read about but had never seen, had dreamed about but had never dreamed I would see: dandelions, apples, snow, spring in England's shires, the white cliffs of Dover. In his eyes my body, me, was everything I dreamed of becoming.

That was your father before any of you were a twinkle in his eye. More accurately, that was my lover and then my husband. Your father was a different man altogether. Suddenly a stranger occupied my bed. His tongue now turned to wood. All the laughter of my sisters, the halfhearted curses of my mother, my father's promise of blue misery, all came true in this strange man, this father, this latter-day husband and lover.

I saw the change in him. My hands were full with you children. He went out of reach. He cradled you as if he didn't know which side was up, which down. He held you at arm's length to avoid the tar and feathers of you babies. Soon I earned the same treatment, but if you children were tar and feathers, I was refuse. His face creased when he came near me. What had become of my silk skin? My precious features disappeared into my face, earning neither praise nor blame—just his silence, his wooden tongue, and that bad-smell look of his. I kept quiet for as long as I could. I watched him retreat from all of us, hoping he'd reel himself back in, since the line between us was strong and I thought unbreakable; but no. I had to shout to get him to hear me. I shouted like my mother standing at the upstairs window to some rude stranger in the street twenty-five yards away. I sounded like my father filling the door frame. My jeering sisters insinuated their way into my voice. And your father simply kept walking away.

Believe me, I pulled my hair and beat the ground with my hands and feet to get at him in my head and in the ground he walked on that I worshiped. Hadn't he delivered England to me and all the seasons of England, all England's shires and the fog he'd left out of his serenades, no doubt just to keep some surprise in store for me? The first morning I opened the door that autumn and shouted "Fire!" when I saw all that smoke, thinking the whole street on fire, all the streets, London burning, and slammed the door and ran into his arms and his laughter, and he took me out into it in my nightdress, he in his pajamas, and all the time I followed him, not ashamed to be seen outside in my thin, flimsy nylon (if anyone could see through that blanket) because he was in his pajamas, the blue striped ones, and his voice, his sweet drone, told me it was fine, this smoke without fire was fine, "This is fog."

He walked away and everything started to be erased by that fog. That smoke without fire crossed the ocean into my past and obliterated Kitty, Georgetown, the house on William Street, everything he had touched, every place I had known him in. I swallowed that fog. It poured into my ears, nose, eyes, mouth. He was gone. I got a chest pain and breathlessness that made me panic. There wasn't just me. There were you children. I had to breathe for you children. The pain in my chest that was your father had to be plucked out, otherwise I too would be lost to you all, and to myself.

▲

The first time I see him is the last time I see him. I can't wait to get to the front of the queue to have him all to myself. When I get there, my eyes travel up and down his body. From those few gray hairs that decorate his temples and his forehead and his nose to the cuffs at his ankles and sparkling black shoes. He wears a black suit, a double-breasted number with three brass buttons on the cuff of each sleeve. He lies on his back with his hands clasped over his flat stomach. There is too much powder on his face. Let's get out of this mournful place, Dad. We have a lot of catching up to do. He has the rare look—of holding his breath, of not breathing, in between inhaling and exhaling—that exquisitely beautiful corpses capture. For a moment after I invite him to leave with me, I expect his chest to inflate, his lids to open, and those clasped hands to unfold and pull him upright into a sitting position, as if he really were just napping because he has dressed way too early for the ball.

▲

There are myths about this sort of thing. Father enslaves son. Son hates father, bides his time, waits for the strong father to weaken. Son pounces one day, pounces hard and definite, and the father is overwhelmed, broken, destroyed with hardly any resistance, except that of surprise and then resignation. Son washes his hands but finds he is washing hands that are not bloodstained, not marked or blemished in any way. He is simply scrubbing hands that no longer belong to him—they are his father's hands, attached to his arms, his shoulders, his body. He has removed a shadow all the more to see unencumbered the father in himself. There is the widow he has made of his mother. He cannot love her as his father might. While his father lived, he thought he could. The moment his father expired, he knew his mother would remain unloved.

I alight too soon from a number 53 bus on Blackheath Hill, disembark while the bus is moving, and stumble, trip from two legs onto all fours, hands like feet, transforming, sprouting more limbs, becoming a spider and breaking my fall. That same fall is now a tumble, a dozen somersaults that end with me standing upright and quite still on two legs with the other limbs dangling. Onlookers, who fully expected disaster, applaud. I walk back up the hill to the block of council flats as a man might, upright, on two legs. My other limbs dangle, swing as if they are two hands. Some days I will be out of breath, I will gasp and exhale, and the cloud before me will be not my winter's breath but the silken strands of a web or, worse, fire. Other days I might look at a bed of geraniums planted on the council estate and turn all their numberless petals into stone. A diamond held between my thumb and index finger crumbles in this mood, in this light, like the powdery wings of a butterfly.

I stare out of an apartment on the twenty-fourth floor of a tower block overlooking the nut-brown Thames. That wasp on the windowpane nibbling up and down the glass for a pore to exit through, back into the air and heat, tries to sting what it can feel but cannot see. My father is the window. I am the wasp. Sometimes a helping hand comes along and lifts the window, and the wasp slides out. Other times a shadow descends, there is a displacement of air, and it is the last thing the wasp knows. Which of those times is this? I want to know. I don't want to know. I am not nibbling nor trying to sting. I am kissing, repeatedly, rapidly, the featureless face of my father. It feels like summer light. It reflects a garden. Whose is that interfering hand? Why that interrupting shadow? My child's hand. My child's shadow. My son or my father? My son and my father. Two sons, two fathers. Yet three people. We walk behind a father's name, shoulder a father's memory. Wear another's walk, another's gait. Wait for what has happened to their bodies, the same scars, maladies, aches, to surface in ours.

I want to shed my skin. Walk away from my shadow. Leave my name in a place I cannot return to. To be nameless, bodiless. To swim to Wallace Stevens's Key West, which is shoreless, horizonless. Blackheath Hill becomes Auden's Bristol Street, an occasion for wonder and lament. Blackheath at 5:45 on a foggy winter morning becomes Peckham Rye. There are no trees on Blackheath, but angels hang in the air, if only Blake were there to see them. On the twenty-fourth floor towering above the Thames, water, not land, surrounds me. Everything seems to rise out of that water. Look up at ambling clouds and the tower betrays its drift out to sea.

Honorée Fanonne Jeffers

The Tail of Color

My father goes off to work in the morning three times a week to teach at the mostly white university in the next town over. He is the only black faculty member in the English department and began working at this school when we moved to North Carolina. The four women of the house compete to take care of him, pour his juice, hug the cheek he can't seem to shave smooth enough. He laughs at our hovering and calls us by our special nicknames. Mine is from a poem by Dunbar: "Little Brown Baby wif de sparklin' eyes / Set on your pappy's knee." He kisses each of our hands before he leaves in the best of moods, whistling jazz tunes.

My six-year-old mind can't understand the alchemy that transforms my father from the charming man who declares he loves only us—he is the sweetest man in the world, the smartest man—into the danger he presents to that house of women, when the thin shell of his good will peels away. In the morning, my father is the husband of us all, and his women are so hopeful. When he returns in the evening from work, he will be hard to his women: my mother, my two older sisters, me. He'll snatch food from our plates with his unwashed fingers and dare us to say anything. He'll forget the sweetness of names, calling us other ugly words that make us know he hates us for letting him down. No more kissing of our small hands. He knows well our fears.

"You know, you're too fat," he says to me, ignoring his own girth. "No wonder you have no friends. You're never going to be as pretty as your sisters when you grow up, no matter how hard you try."

"Now this one," this to my middle sister, Sisi, "you're pretty. In fact, you're too pretty, too yellow, and not at all smart. I hope you can find a husband. You're not good for much else."

Or, to my mother, "You think I don't know why you married me?" A question, but never with an answer.

Most of those evenings, Mama tries never to leave him alone with us. She knows he becomes more vicious when he doesn't have her as an audience. Nearby, she hovers in the background, her eyes aware and poised, then she steps in between him and us, deflecting the blows of his words. "Go upstairs, sugar, go on, now," she will say to us, and we will run, run, even as he orders us back. "You have not been excused. Come back here, I said! Do you hear me? I am the man here. I am!" And, at first, she will speak his name like the soothing of oil. "Lance, Lance. Baby, stop it now."

The shouting between them will go on into the night, drifting upstairs to me and my sisters, to where we listen at the heating vents leading to the rooms below us. The crying of my father, exposed like that of a very small child.

The next morning, my father will sleep late, and when I come home from school, his office door will be closed, and he is typing his poems, his mood ruined for good the rest of the week, no matter how much we try.

When I am a woman, after my father is dead, I will remember living in the house with my father meant fear of those whites in the place my father went. Whatever happened, when my mother and sisters and I tried to make him happy, dangling ourselves in front of him like decorations on a Christmas tree, my father did not know he was worthy.

Who are these white people who keep me from making him

happy? They must be different from my teacher at my own school, who smiles at me and gives me extra snacks after lunch. Her face flushes pink in pleasure at the high marks on my papers. She strokes my hair when she walks through the aisles of children. Who are these other white people my father sees three times a week? Whoever they are, I have to protect him from them. If he is cruel, I need to know how to change that cruelty into goodness. I can never become angry at him or fight back because first I have to take care of him. I have to shield him from what blinds him.

The color of my mother blinds him. The shades of meaning in the skin of a black, black woman walking among the yellow idols of my father's family. They knew their own truth: God does not forgive certain sins like the blackness of my mother. She can breathe now that every one of them is dead. The final son, her husband, is dead, and my mother can be a proud widow, traveling through the mistakes of manners and history, hoping no one notices. She can ask her brown daughter's advice now and never have to look again over her shoulder at her in-laws who expect her to fail.

I learn, in unspoken ways, after my daddy is dead, that when I tell any stories, I should not forget my mother's life. Her life was full before she met him, before my sisters and I came along. I should not forget to talk about the red clay of her home and the slave shack that used to stand on the now vacant ground. I should not forget the stripes and flowers of her brothers' and sisters' clothes made from cheap fabric remnants or sometimes flour sacking. I should not forget the pickings of peaches, plums, and cotton when she was young, earning money for her store-bought underwear and sanitary napkins; nor the newness of the books she read in college—"*Brand* new!"—and how they felt in her already roughened hands. There was no marking of "colored" in the front of these books, and no one prepared her for this joy. And I should not forget her first sight of a real bathtub when she was in college, and how she began to bathe so many times a day that she rubbed her skin raw.

She went against the advice of her own mother who said she had the gift for hair, could start a real beauty shop, not stand for six hours over someone else's hot plate or the gas eye of someone else's stove. Instead she would make a life as a black businesswoman in Eatonton, Georgia (maybe the first one; my mother doesn't know), not a life of scrubbing a white somebody's drawers for the rest of her life and pretending to smile while doing it. Scrubbing drawers or wiping little white noses, or both, was the only job a poor black woman, "a black, black woman," could get when my mother was a young girl. There was a time when the white women of the town factory officially protested against integration because they needed someone to look after their homes while they were out seeking their own liberation. Who better than a black woman to clean their kitchens and newly installed indoor toilets and to look after their white children while they worked the assembly line? They needed someone who would dote permanently on their little ones, and all for ten dollars a week.

My mother says that from the beginning her mother was never proud of her. She was too dark, her nose too broad, her hair too nappy. Grandma found no pleasure in being the mother of a foolish, dark girl who wanted to waste her time on college. Why should my mother need to go to college only to return after four years, to work the same job as every other black woman? Better for her to work for herself than to face that day, surely down the line, when one of those factory women's husbands would ask her to take an extra dollar a week—"and don't forget those leftovers!"—for a little night-work. And surely down the line would come the day she might meet a moist gaze and gently pry little pink fingers from her own darker ones, go home, and have to solve the problem of her children's hunger. Or surely would come the day when she might come home late, bringing sweet-and-sour candy for her dark children to suck, turn her back to her husband in bed, ignoring his confusion.

In college, my mother held books during the week, a straightening comb on Friday nights and all day Saturday through those four years, charging fifty cents from the moneyed and lighter, more acceptable girls who were middle class, whose fathers were doctors, lawyers, insurance salesmen, Pullman porters, whose mothers, of course, even lighter than the fathers, were teachers, social workers, housewives. Fifty cents for a regular or hard press with the metal heated comb. First the oil to protect the scalp and hair, then the hot comb, then the round irons clicking between my mother's fingers as she stood over a hot plate in her room and made beauty. Always the sound and smell of heat.

I should not forget my mother standing next to the hot plate, talking to her customers in a deadly, cheerful voice. I should not forget how she ignored her own mother and went to college, met and married my father, the progeny of almost-never slaves. My father thought her exotic, a dark woman raised in that old slave shack, so he took her across the country to meet his parents. I should not forget that my father was a man who had never put his fingers in a woman's hair and come away with grease coating his nails.

My father insisted there was not much of a story to his family. His story was just a simple cliché: miscegenation. Lust or love maybe, convenience or rape more likely, in those unions between black female slaves and white masters. Their consequential children were pushed into freedom long before Mister Lincoln came along. The lucky and the mostly pale ones. And decades later, came the important details: my mother and father meeting on the coolness of academic grass, where they read books together in English or French. Nothing else, not really. What was he ashamed to say to my mother and his three daughters, especially me, the darkest one? That those who looked like my mother, his wife, had worked the fields right until Jubilee, and sometimes for years afterward, if their masters weren't kind enough to inform them of their manumission?

My mother would not release him from his family; so reluctantly, he told my sisters and me the basics about his pale mother, Dorothy, and her equally pale husband, Forest, my father's stepfather. Once Dorothy had been married (for how long we don't know) to a very dark man, Henry, my father's father. (We met Henry, the dark man, only once. I was three, and we rode in a car for what seemed like months, to a state where it was cold and the trees were outlined in gray. Henry took me on his lap and kissed me and said I was a pretty, pretty baby girl. We met Henry where trains passed by.) Henry had married Dorothy when she became pregnant, and they lived in a small flat, one room or two. One day, Dorothy's own father, George, a nearly-white man, a doctor, married to a white woman, came to take her only child away. She followed and stayed with her child for a little while.

The one memory given freely by my father, worn smooth in his mind from constant use, was of Mertina, his grandfather George's white wife. Sometimes my father would talk of her on those days he returned from teaching. A courageous woman, going against the racist and lawful tide to marry her black doctor, a woman smelling cool and of flowers that did not grow in the Nebraska wilderness. The kindest woman on earth. A nurse, working with his grandfather, the only doctor in Stromsburg, Nebraska. She holds my father, a toddler, in a picture I will see after his death; in another picture, she guides the huge horse he rides on and looks up carefully from the ground.

There were only a few people in Daddy's family: some appropriately colorless; no children for those who were terrified that the blood from across the water might show up again, a freakish joke of the Creator. My father's family tree was first tainted with the copper brown of the patriarch, the great-great grandfather, but he can be forgiven. He was a doctor who sired a doctor. Who begot who begot.

For years my father's people watched the skin of his three children for signs of darkening and then they decided. "All these children, Trellie," my mother was told, "they have to stop sometime—don't you think?"

The weekend of Mother's Day, I try calling my grandmother, Dorothy. I sit waiting on the phone for nearly twenty minutes. The housekeeper tells me, "Mrs. Jeffers no here" and puts down the phone. I wait and check my watch as the time passes. One dime.

Two dimes. Finally, I hear my stepgrandfather, over ninety himself, walking heavily down the stairs to tell me that Dorothy died two weeks before. There was a cremation, no ceremony, and they didn't want to bother us. My mother hovers in the background until I hang up in tears. She wants me to call back. There must be some mistake.

A week later, Dorothy's pictures arrive from California, pasted onto the thick black paper of old albums, a triangle at each corner of the photographs. My grandparents bequeathed all the rest of their belongings and money to friends of theirs. Only the pictures are left, and Mama imagines that she should give them to my sisters and me. She asks how she should preserve the photographs that were printed on delicate paper nearly a century ago. "Your sisters don't want them; do you?" she asks. "I would think you should want them. If they were my family...." Perhaps she should save them for her grandchildren. May these children of her children never be cursed with darkness and hidden away.

I am startled at images of Dorothy as a baby or a child, or together with Daddy's stepfather as a young couple in stiff, stylized poses. In every one, Dorothy looks light enough to pass for white, her hair waving only so slightly away from her forehead, the lashes long and thick on the slanted eyes. It strikes me that she is identical to my sister, Sisi, as a little girl, when her face would wrinkle in tears, pink underneath the buttermilk, when I shouted at her.

Mama taps another picture of Dorothy, this time as a young girl wearing long, lace-edged bloomers and camisole. "Ain't Sisi the spit of her? When Sisi was a baby, folks used to ask me was she my own. I told them, 'No, I'm just carrying around this big ole child, hurting my back cause I'm crazy.' Now you? You were a pretty brown thing. I used to call you 'Mommy's little representative.' I didn't have to prove to anybody you were mine." Mama taps the picture again, her finger dark against Dorothy's pale skin.

Mama carefully flips the pictures over when she is done looking at each one so as not to tear the thin paper. After all, they will be mine soon. She stops and makes a noise of deep satisfaction when she sees a face that doesn't match the others at all, "Umph."

This is a woman much darker, brown, with curly hair like me. "Kinky," my white friends would call it. A five-foot-two woman in Kansas or Arkansas—my mother doesn't know which—with knuckles gripped tight around her two small and pale children's hands. Knuckles ready to pull the trigger on white men, KKK, riding on horses, arriving in the middle of the night at her home to kill her black doctor husband who had refused earlier that morning to step off the town sidewalk for a white man. I imagine the riders licking their lips at the thought of a black woman alone in the house. Oh so easy this would be for them. They can already feel the clench of her buttocks, her long skirts pulled up over her face to make sure God isn't watching. Her back down on the floor of a house far too grand for a black man to have built, even if he was a fair-skinned doctor, and they would take her. All respectability would be gone. Out there alone without her man: the black doctor they don't know she had begged to hide beneath the house in the cellar. It would be so easy to snatch away her calm, to burn the grand house afterward. So easy until the brown woman does indeed go crazy on them, screaming steady curses. She scares them, this small dark woman with a rifle in her hands, and incredibly, they turn their horses around.

On the back of this picture, her name is printed in block letters, LELA GEORGIA. This is not Mertina, the brave white one who married a black man. This is another woman, a black woman who looks just like what she is. Her husband, who was quickly convinced that her rape was better than his own death, crawled from beneath the floorboards and looked at the wild eyes of his dark wife, at the rifle in her hands. He'd leave her for another woman one day.

He leaves her for the kindest woman on earth, the white woman, Mertina, who watches my father so carefully in those fragile pictures, who loves my daddy so dearly, who surely will take care of him until he becomes a man. She waits until her black doctor husband is dead, buried under hard Nebraska dirt. She waits until the doctor's will is probated and the land and house and respectability belong to her. A month later she places a tag around the wrist of my father, the precious child, and mails him on a train back to his almost-white mother, Dorothy, and her husband. She waited and then peeled away my father's nine-year-old heart. She peeled his heart away layer by layer and left the cold inside for me.

"Nothing goes over a mule's back that don't buckle under his belly."

Almost thirty years ago in San Francisco, my mother sat on the couch in the living room of my father's parents' house and felt the chill of their dogged politeness in the face of her darkness. I want to say Mama decided to stay married to my father only when she saw the picture of Lela Georgia, the doctor's first wife, sitting on the mantel. That brown woman was dead then, and so was the doctor, and so was his second, white wife. Perhaps through twenty-eight years of marriage, Lela Georgia, not my sisters and me, is the biggest reason Mama stayed with a man who looked more like the enemy than someone she loved.

I should not forget the color of my mother, of my father, of his people, of her people, who are my people.

So at the end of this story, at the beginning of my own, will I talk about the hue of my skin, about the wriggling tail of color, showing through history? And at what point should I say there will be dark women looking at me, always, their lips pressed together, a warning?

Gwendolyn Brooks

Keziah

On Tuesday, March 14, 1978, at eight in the evening, two weeks after her ninetieth birthday, my mother stopped.

Keziah Corinne Wims Brooks.

She had been healthy most of her life. She had been a fast walker, a joyously rhythmic little walker, most of her life. Most mornings, her waking was with pleasure in the new prospects, pleasure in new planning. She was an alert contributor to the procedures of her milieu.

In 1976 she had published, happily, her book of memories, her impressions, with a couple of fictions. She had insisted on calling it *The Voice, and Other Short Stories*. She had insisted on paying for its publication, out of her own savings. I gave her an autographing party at Chicago's South Side Community Art Center. Many attended, many spoke in tribute to her. Her last sister, Beulah, came from Topeka to assist her. Seven hundred fifty dollars' worth of books were sold! She gave a speech, reading it with precise distinctness, precise delight. (I remembered that, a few years earlier, she had given an impressive speech at a Metropolitan Community Church celebration in a downtown hotel with no paper in front of her, amazing the throng with her self-possession and soft dignity.) At this party, she enjoyed the refreshments, the piano music, the flowers. And there was a wide big-lettered banner across the gallery:

CONGRATULATIONS, MRS. KEZIAH BROOKS!

Ke-ZI-ah. I have always loved my mother's name. ("Corinne"

she had given to herself.) And I love her nickname, "Kip," which, strangely, she didn't care for.

There had been that strange sorrow of losing her only son, my brother Raymond, in 1974. But that sorrow did not prove flattening; it was not such as could persuade her to Resign; Hoke Norris' *Chicago Sun-Times* article on her reported her as saying she didn't have "a worry in the world!"—this, at the age of eighty-nine. Interestingly and sadly, by the time that article appeared, on January 22, 1978, Hoke, novelist and *Sun-Times* book editor, had died, and my mother saw it, rather hazily, in the hospital. I taped it to the wall above her narrow bed at Michael Reese. The Michael Reese doctors and nurses were impressed.

There had been the Robbery. *That* was *almost* flattening. That happened on a particularly joyous Sunday morning in the spring of 1977. My husband and I had taken her to a nice restaurant for brunch, after a grocery-shopping trip. I remember her very special happiness. She couldn't praise enough the food that she ate with such delight, nor the attractiveness of the room; nor my "kindness," as she chose to call it, in taking her on the financed shopping trip, although this was an almost regular happening. After the little festivity—she considered restaurant visits singular specialties—we took her home. As a rule, my husband, on arrival at her door, would see her into and through the house. But on this occasion, because I was leaving, immediately, for the airport, with just enough time to make my plane, he saw her through the door only. A couple of hours after my arrival at the campus I'd flown to, my agent called, with the news that my mother's home had been robbed during our brunch absence—robbed of all those articles a thief can sell easily: phonograph, radio, television set, electric fans, etc. I called my mother. By that time, my husband had "secured" her with a repaired and barred back door and dining room door. She was dazed. Such a violation! To think! Strangers moving around in Her House, handling Her Things! She couldn't get over it! The police were called. They apprehended no one, although neighbors told us it had been the work of three brothers on the block, three brothers who subsequently went to jail for another robbery in the area.

Invasion. She couldn't get over it.

She never did get over it. We spelled her decline from the moment of that invasion. It wasn't long before she began to lose interest in food. Although very slender all her life, she had loved food, selecting it, cooking it, daintily eating the products of the recipes she had collected over the years. But after the invasion, I might return from a lecture trip, laden with gift groceries, and find no evidence that anything had been eaten since my departure. I would find only the little gray-green sculptured cup, from which she liked to drink water, on the kitchen sink. The icebox would seem undisturbed.

"Aren't you eating, Mama?"

"Yes, I'm eating."

"Well, I went to Stop and Shop and got you some *wonderful* lamb chops."

"Oh, thank you!"

But she got thinner and thinner.

Then one Sunday in October something happened that alarmed her as well as ourselves. I had told her I'd go to church with her that Sunday. Always, on such an occasion, she would be charmingly dressed and at the window watching for us, waiting. This time, I had to ring the doorbell, then knock knock knock at the door, and at the vacant window, repeatedly, before attracting her attention. Finally she came to the door in her nightgown and robe. She seemed bewildered, but when I mentioned church, and told her that Henry was in the car, ready to drive us down, she suddenly remembered what she had entirely forgotten. She was abject, contrite. She couldn't forgive herself. She began immediately to "collect" herself, and in no time she was neat and ready to go. Yet, nothing like that had ever happened before, and she was truly alarmed.

That was the last Sunday she ever went to church.

Something else disturbed us. Always willing to be chatty, always responsive to what others had to say—she had always listened attentively to the ideas and opinions of others, and had responded with eager liveliness—she became increasingly silent.

I asked her, over and over, to live with me. My house was about thirty blocks south of hers. I told her I would expand my five-room cottage so that she could have her own quarters, her privacy. She wouldn't come. She loved her home. She wanted to live alone. She had stopped renting out her second floor, because she wanted "peace and quiet." Once, during this time, her furnace, tampered with by one of those professional tamperers, one of those roving "furnace-fixers" I had warned her against, exploded. Fortunately, my husband and I were visiting her at the time. It was a very cold winter night. We bundled her up and insisted, of course, that she come to our house, until I could get a new furnace installed in her basement. I'll never forget her poignant "I *wish* I could stay home!" as we helped her down the snowy steps.

I had a new furnace installed, and she came back to her precious home. She proceeded with her steady decline. She ate less and less. Soon, she Wasn't Well. That is the way to put it. Yes, she was eighty-nine, but for Keziah Wims Brooks to be Not Well was strange.

Because, although she was weak and, finally, had to stay in bed (except for going to the bathroom—two rooms and a rough road of strain away), all we could observe, in the way of wrongness, was that she was not eating.

I moved in with her. I called the office of her doctor. Edward Beasley, a highly-respected pediatrician, was doctor to all of us. He had seen both my children through sniffles, measles, and chicken pox. When, many years before, I had decided my heart was "failing," he had seen me through the fantasy. "He's dead," said a woman at the other end of the line. Very carefully, I gave my mother that news. "That's—shocking," she said, with precise quiet. She meant those words exactly. It was, as they say, "the end of an era."

I had to hunt up another doctor. Val Gray Ward told me that a Fred Daniels was willing to make house calls. Mama seemed to trust him. She allowed him to influence her into a neighborhood clinic, a clinic on 43rd Street near King Drive. She had told me she did not want to go to "any hospital." And she had written up a little document that stated "in no uncertain terms" (an old phrase of hers) that she wanted NO OPERATIONS. She was so weak on the day of her visit to the clinic that Henry had to carry her in. Dr. Daniels was able to convince her that she must go to a hospital for examination and treatment. She listened to him with polite concern. She looked at me, then, and said another poignancy: "Well, I'll just have to rely on your judgment."

Responsibility. I was, from that moment, entirely Responsible for my mother—bills, care, chores, decisions.

She entered Michael Reese. A couple of days after she was settled in there I read to her a piece I had written on an Amtrak train—Tuesday, November 29, 1977. Narrow in her narrow hospital bed, very still, she listened attentively to my assessment, clumsy and innocent (and criminally inadequate, as I later knew) of her voyages, her countries found. Then she said, with acceptance round and gentle, "That's *nice*."

I had always wanted a "simple" I-love-you from my mother. I do not remember any. I have no memory of volunteered motherly hugs and kisses in any department of our life together. In adulthood, I would hug her on arrivals and departures. She would respond with apparent pleasure and participation. But displays of affection were not spontaneous. (My own children I squeezed, kissed, grabbed on sudden impulse. Even when she was two, I was forever looping up my little daughter and carrying her from one end of the house to the other; she was almost like a doll; "Why don't you put that child down?" my husband would say.)

Yet my mother's affections, we all knew, were present and clear. As daughter, as sister, as mother, as wife, as grandmother, as neighborhood friend, she was subscriptive and serious and yielding.

After her death, I found in the treasured old desk she had inherited, from her brother Will, a notebook in which she had inscribed gift paragraphs to her eight inheritors. Her elegant handwriting! Nothing else was in that 10½-inch by 8-inch fifty-sheet blue notebook, called by its commercial creators "*Sterling Quality*." My gift, "To Gwendolyn," was:

Dear Daughter,

I am truly appreciative of your many kind deeds. They have given me much comfort and happiness. I hope your success continues and that you will be happy throughout life.

Love, Mama.

I have` never been one to put much stock in *dreams*. But—how pleasingly marvelous it is that we see, after their deaths, mother and father and brother, and sometimes aunts and uncles, in our dreams. As *well* as the thousand-and-three monsters and gargoyles and strangers charming or wan! There they are, semi-coolly or warmly wonderful; physiques, aspects, expressions very much as usual. And INTERESTED in us.

So, I lost and shall never lose my mother. She turns up in dreams, again and again, her mother-eyes regarding me. She says a few words; answers a question; or looks. Just looks.

Here is the testimonial I took to her in the hospital:

In a little poem I have written about my mother, I have noted the particulars of her character. The poem commends my mother's essential strength. Keziah Corinne Wims Brooks was and is a courageous woman. It has never occurred to her that she should slink away from any of the challenges of life. The challenges of life— the agonies, sorrows, the million and ten frustrations, perplexities, problems, reductions, dominations, and expulsions—*she* has looked at with a calculating eye, has judged, has catalogued. She has tamed what had to be tamed, what could, what should be tamed. She has adjusted to whatever rocks were super-ornery, determinedly smoothing the edges of such rocks so that she might sit *bearably* thereon. No fear, no fight, no fury has been so oppressive as to leave her weaponless. Even now, in her eighty-ninth year, when certain details of this New Time begin, shockingly, to seem unconquerable (home invasion, cruelty to the very old and the very young, our accelerating human coldness), she has thought of a way of redress: she is proceeding into the depths of herself, where it is warm and cozy, receptive, comfortable. From these depths, into which her friends cannot follow her, she waves with a genial pleasantness, but she says very little, and she will not let us pull her out. Withdrawal, then, is her Last Weapon. So far as *she* is concerned, it works. It is a resource that works.

This change in her—alarming to us—dates from October of 1977. The home invasion in the preceding spring had shaken her fundamentally. Her loved television set, a gift from her daughter, had been stolen, her doors splintered in the forced entry during, luckily, her absence. In October, her heating plant failed, and even though assured it would be replaced, somehow her faith in her ability to control her environment began to waver.

About the new silences (due partly, I think, to fear of forgetfulness and partly to a willingness to learn from the busytalk of others, and partly to I know not what)—I am reminded of some very wise lines of the Fugitivist poet Merrill Moore:

> ... *silence* is not death.
> It merely means that the one who is conserving breath
> is not concerned with tattle and small
> quips.

Poem:

My Mother
Of Keziah Corinne Wims Brooks;
Of yesterday's strength.

My mother sits in yesterday
and teeters toward today
and topples toward tomorrow's edge
and panics back away.

Yesterday taught her to contrive
to dreg-up and to thoroughlize.
—Fitting her for Some reckonings
with the not-old and with surprise.

(December, 1975)

Yes, my mother, born March 1, 1888, is a *daughter* of yesterday. She has always been, however, willing to sally forth, albeit cautiously, to test or question today's new thing, today's strange thing. She is even willing, as I've implied here, to topple toward an exhilarating, tentative, almost mischievous little combat with the hints, science, promises, problems, and affronts of tomorrow; but, her steady intelligence tells her, the waters of tomorrow are indeed too deep, too deep for her, and she "panics back away," leaving the larger risks of tomorrow for the solving hands of the young. Even so, she has certain lessons to hand down to the young—certain positives that, she believes, were reliable yesterday, are reliable today, and will be reliable tomorrow unless we humankind are going to start from scratch with new gods, new earth, new sky, new exits and entrances, and an absolute revolution, or reversal of decisions. Yesterday taught my mother to go down to the very roots of things, the very roots of life, thoroughness, that dutiful calm determination to be Equal to this life, to this world that has made it possible for her to face—cleanly, deliberately, reasonably—with "innocent" and steady eyes—whatever comes, whatever rises before her.

My mother "brought up" my late brother Raymond and myself in the sunshine of certain rules. One: We must be clean of body; she scrubbed us vigorously until we children could satisfy her high standards of cleanliness. That was *outside*! As for cleanliness inside, long before it was fashionable to consider diet with strict seriousness, she was so inclined. Our meals were healthful, inclusive, attractive, controlled. Two: We must be dutiful. Dutifulness has always been her major concept. "Always do the Right Thing." Three: We must empathize with other people. She was fond of quoting her own mother, Luvenia Wims—"If you know yourself, you know *other people*." Four: We must respect ourselves. Our bodies were monuments of purity and beauty and we were not to poison them with filth of any kind, with disrespect of any kind. Our minds were clean and shining crystal, into which we were to pour only what was clean and bright and good. Five: We must respect the honor of Family—in the smaller sense our Family of Four plus our scattered relatives-in-the-large (although she would not have expressed it in this way), our Family of the Black millions all over the world. We must put no disgrace on Family. Six: We must work for what we use and enjoy. To steal—the merest match or marble or licorice switch—*unthinkable*! Other people's property is sacredly theirs. (And, it follows, *ours* is sacredly ours.) Seven: We must be polite and helpful to other people. This meant each of us must meet all, friend, stranger, with a pleasant face; a nod, a salutation. This meant, until such behavior in Chicago became perilous, allowing the hungry unknown to sit at table; or giving a dollar here, a dollar there—often ill-afforded. Eight: As long as we were children and controllable, we must go to church and respect God and Godliness. Godliness was a combination of decency, kindliness, and the observance of Duty.

These mother-charms—abetted by my father's underwriting concern, protection, and reliable love—are the good to which I continue referral, and which I consider my continuing nutrition.

Thank you, Mama.

Della Taylor Scott

My Country 'Tis of Thee

In my family, we avoid talking about those dreadful years when my father was a sergeant in the army and when we had to move from the South to the North. As we reminisce, we pretend as though our eyes never saw stars and stripes blowing in the wind or proud uniformed men marching to the rhythm of drumbeats. We pretend that we never heard my father's exaggerated war stories and his heartfelt song, "My Country 'Tis of Thee."

I have few fond memories of my childhood during the early 1960s in Killeen, Texas. After that, life with my patriotic father began to deteriorate. We lived on a military base in McNair Village, in a yellowish apartment complex encircled by sunburned lawns and hilly grass fields, where armadillos in their shiny coats roamed. We were one of the few black families living among neighbors who were Anglos or of Mexican, Irish, and Italian descent. Although the South was segregated, we were not aware of Jim Crow laws until a few years later. My father and mother got along well with our white neighbors. Usually on Saturday afternoons my father would drive a group of us to the theater, next to the commissary. With our friends, my older sister, brother, and I would sit in the front row eating our puffed pink cotton candy. Being in the front row always made us feel as though we were in the film. The lights dimmed. Within seconds, we were in *Cinderfella* with Jerry Lewis. We'd snicker every time

Jerry blundered. "What a nut," we would say. He was the biggest fool we had ever seen. After the flick, we'd race home under the glistening bright sun, whooping and hollering. Once we arrived home, my brother and I would grab either our bikes or roller skates. Or we'd put on our Roy Rogers and Dale Evans cowboy hats, and our holsters with cap guns. We'd wander throughout the neighborhood with our friends until dinnertime. As soon as we'd eat, we'd rush back outside until we heard either the sounds of crickets or the voice of my mother, who threatened to skin us alive with her freshly-cut switch.

On the Fourth of July, my father always insisted that we attend a special event on the base. Together we listened to boring speeches that we wanted to forget. To make matters worse, we were forced to listen to the military band play a litany of patriotic songs that made us want to reach for the nearest pillow. "Can we go home now?" we would ask. "Shush," my mother would say. Disgusted, my father's caramel-colored face frowned. "We just got here. I'm not taking you kids nowhere no more." Then my father would turn his head to hear the blaring band play "God Bless America." Standing with his shoulders pulled back in his freshly-ironed khaki uniform, he sang in his tenor voice along with the others as they gazed at their beloved American flag.

Tall and skinny with a thin mustache, my father didn't have dreams of becoming a lieutenant. He didn't have dreams of receiving a Purple Heart. But he had dreams of becoming a well-respected soldier. He thrived on gaining honor from the army and his comrades. He was happiest around his "army buddies," more so than around us. I remember whenever his black soldier friends visited our home, my father, who hardly ever talked to us unless he was giving us orders, would become vivacious. He'd laugh more. Together, he and his friends would all puff on their cigarettes and play Miles Davis albums; they talked about the different bands at the NCO club where my father sometimes played the saxophone. Or they exchanged Korean War stories. My older brother and I would come out to greet the warmhearted men, who were the color of pecans. They always smiled tenderly at us as though we were their own children. Sitting on the arm of their chairs, we would show them our Superman comic books and baseball cards. Sometimes I would teach them how to draw pictures on my red-framed Etch A Sketch.

Whenever my father's white soldier friends came by, he would tell us to "scat" and to stay quiet. When the doorbell rang, we would run upstairs and sit near the banister and listen to their conversation. From a distance, we could see a tattooed arm. Legs crossed. A white hand reaching for an ashtray. My father seemed far more animate around them than he was with his black friends. His voice was louder. More cheerful. He was bursting with energy as if he were high. "Yes, you're right," he kept saying. "You sure do know a lot. How did you get to become such a genius?" He even spoke proper English. If they asked for a glass of water, he moved quickly like a waiter who wanted a good tip. He walked briskly to show them the phone in the kitchen, where my mother was washing the dishes. He gave his white soldier friends the loving attention that we had always wanted from him.

As soon as they left, he yelled, "Y'all can come down now." We walked in the smoke-filled room, where ashes lay on the floor. My father's face still beamed with excitement. By the late evening, he had transformed back into his quiet self. Why did he value his white friends so much? I wondered. Years later I realized that he thought it was a great honor to have white friends who perceived him as a social equal. During the 1920s and 1930s, he was raised in rural Georgia, where he and other black sharecropping families lived in fear of white people.

Unlike my father, my mother, who was raised in South Carolina, preferred to be around blacks, especially her black women friends. I always knew when her friend, Mrs. Griffin, was coming by. Coffee perked. Dishes rattled. Two china cups and saucers sat on the kitchen table. Sugar cubes filled the crystal bowl. Soon the smell of buttered pound cake pervaded the house. Mrs. Griffin, who was the color of cinnamon, was in her thirties. Her breath always smelled like Doublemint gum; she always wore white sleeveless blouses. She and my mother would sit at the kitchen table for hours drinking coffee. Whenever I would come in the room, they would become quiet. My mother, who looked like a black Indian with her high cheekbones, would tell me to look for something. "I can't find my beige scarf with those elephant designs. Find it fo' me," she said. I frantically started my search. After a while I realized that the scarf didn't exist. Once I caught on, I would sit in the next room to eavesdrop. I could hear Mrs. Griffin stirring sugar cubes in her cup. "I'm sick of Larry running around with his army friends. He ain't no damn bachelor." My mother responded, "Why do these army guys put us last and their friends first? I'm tired of it." They'd tell stories about how a neighbor found a 38-D bra on her front steps. Cigarette butts with pink lipstick. Stringy hair on her husband's jacket. Entrapment. A familiar story. Where could the military wives go with a house full of children?

A few months later, I remember my father announced that he would be stationed in Germany. He was still in his thirties and was glad to gain more respect from his peers. My mother refused to go to Germany where the Holocaust had occurred. Instead, we moved to Atlanta where my father's younger twelve brothers and sister lived. As children, we adored them, because they talked with us. They gave us the attention that we never received from our father. They would come by our apartment on Booker T. Washington Drive, which was just a few blocks away from Morehouse College. From our aunts and uncles, we learned about Martin Luther King, Jr. Protests. Marches. Medgar Evers. "We Shall Overcome." On Saturdays, my uncles would stop by to bring us candy. Sometimes we'd watch *Wagon Train* or *Rawhide* with them. Or together we'd play Monopoly. We always looked forward to going to their spacious homes for birthday parties and cookouts. Whenever we saw our uncles actually talking and playing cards with their sons and daughters, we envied their relationships. Why couldn't we have a loving father? We simply wanted to forget about our father who was on the other side of the world.

Sometimes my mother would receive thin, blue air-mail letters from my father. She would insist that we write to him. But what could we say? I would write a short letter that sounded more like a form letter. There wasn't any emotion. My older sister, who was now in high school, felt the same way. "I'm not going to write," she said. "He doesn't care about us." Within a few months, he wrote to my mother to let us know that he was going to be on furlough. He would be in Atlanta for a week or so. We were not excited. Before we knew it, he arrived all dressed up in his wool green uniform and hat. We could smell the familiar odor of Vitalis on his hair. He expected us to whoop and holler, but we couldn't. And we wouldn't. I remember watching him grab our mother, who was thrilled to see him; they embraced one another for a long time. But we could not reach out to him. Secretly we wanted to tell him to go back to Germany. With his face beaming, he hugged us tightly.

After a year passed, my father received orders that he would be stationed in Boston. We didn't want to leave Atlanta, after living in a dream for two years. It was 1965, and it would be our first time in the North. We moved to Tarrant Lane in Wakefield, an all-white suburban town where there was a cluster of military houses near a highway. The white folks were as cold as their icy winters. We simply were not welcomed. In the stores on the Wakefield-Reading line, my brother and I were watched and followed as if we had just escaped from a Georgia chain gang. When we went out on

Halloween, wearing our masks, the neighbors shut their doors in our faces, as soon as they saw our brown hands. We had never seen so much hatred. I remember Bill Russell, the Celtics basketball star who lived in Reading, was being harassed by his white neighbors.

Nevertheless, my father loved his job in Boston, where he continued to work as a sergeant; he was in charge of supplies for all of the army recruits. He had two white soldiers reporting to him. To him, he had now made great progress. He never thought that whites would be saying "Yes, sir" to him. Usually, he would come home in a good mood. But still he didn't say much to us. After dinner, he'd sit in his favorite chair across from the television and read the *Record American*. He'd have a cup of coffee and a cigarette. He and my mother would talk about the Boston Strangler, Richard Speck, the man who killed several nurses. My mother, who was normally upbeat, usually complained about the neighborhood. "We're in the middle of nowhere," she would say. "If I had known that we would be isolated like this, I wouldn't have come up here." After a while, they began to argue. About money. Bills. Household finance. Sears. Not owning a home. Not having enough food at the end of the month. "What are you spending your money on?" my mother asked. "You've been in the army almost twenty years, and we ain't got nothing to show for it." They cursed. Doors slammed. Dinner wasn't cooked. Soon my father stopped coming home at night.

One day after coming home from school, to my surprise, my mother said: "We're going to Baltimore to see my sister. Pack up your things." I stared at her long black Indian face. "When are we coming back?" I asked. "I'm not sure." My older sister, who was always feisty, said: "Good. I hope we never come back." While my father was at work, a neighbor drove us to South Station. We hopped on a train and headed back down South. We stayed with my aunt in Baltimore for a week. I remember my father called several times, pleading with my mother to come back. He was afraid that he would be perceived as an unfit husband and father by his army comrades. He vowed and vowed that he would never stay out all night again. We returned and he kept his word.

A year or so later, my father and several of his army friends decided to retire. He had been in the army for twenty years now. He was ashamed because he didn't own any property and he didn't have a savings account. It was important to make up for lost time. His dream now was to get out of debt and to buy a home. He would receive his pension, and we still had access to the army hospitals and commissaries. His cousins in Bridgeport, Connecticut had convinced him that he would be able to find a high-paying job in a major corporation where he could use his skills as an inventory control specialist. Reluctantly we moved to Bridgeport, a depressed city that put us in a gloomy mood.

My father had one disappointment after another. He thought we would be able to rent a spacious house or apartment in the suburbs. But no landlord wanted to rent to a family with three kids. We ended up in a notorious housing project on Trumbull Avenue in Bearsley Terrace, where mean-spirited teenagers pelted us with rocks until we started fighting back and acting like devils. Meanwhile, my father was disappointed because he couldn't find a job as supervisor or as an inventory specialist. He was in his forties. Companies wanted young folks. He ended up working as a security guard at Sikorsky, where his fellow employees ignored him. To them, he was like an old rusty penny on the floor. Nothing. His army buddies who had promised to stay in contact didn't keep their word. He would call them long distance. "Is Sergeant Williams there? Is Sergeant Jackson there? Tell them that Sergeant Taylor called." They didn't return his phone calls. Sometimes his younger brothers and sisters would call from Atlanta. They wanted to visit us. He lied and told them that he played with a band on weekends and would be on the road. My father, who was the oldest in his family, was ashamed of where we lived. Ashamed of himself, he felt like a failure. Shaking his head, he'd read his army retiree newsletters over and over. He grew depressed. To punish himself, he would sit on the sofa and drink two six-packs of Budweiser until he became sloppy drunk.

To rebel against my father, my older sister started following the news about the anti-Vietnam War protests. One day while my father was watching a baseball game on television and drinking his Budweiser, she told us that she was heading to a protest rally. "Where is your flag?" she asked. "We need a flag to burn at our rally." My father jumped up from the sofa as if she had fired a shot at him. "Burn the United States flag? You must be stone crazy. If you burn the flag, you can just forget about coming back in my house. You can just forget it." He paced the floor. My mother stepped in and pleaded with my sister not to go to the rally. "I'm going. And you can't stop me." She slammed the door. "She's going to burn *my* flag." He kept on saying it over and over. In his mind's eye, he pictured the flag in flames. My sister was burning flesh. Blood. She was burning the bodies of soldiers. She was burning his friends who died in World War II and Korea. She was burning his life. *His country.* I had never seen him look devastated. He covered his face with his hands as he sat on the sofa. Close to tears, he turned off the television. His Budweiser no longer tasted good. He just sat on the sofa with his head hung low. My mother tried to soothe him by telling him that my sister was bluffing. Later that evening, my sister walked in as though she had regrets. "We didn't burn your flag." My father just glared at her.

Each day we'd watch the news about how the Vietnam protesters burned their draft cards. How they would lie down in the streets in front of army bases. To our surprise, my father reenlisted in the army; he announced that he would be going to Vietnam. We were all stunned. My mother cried out, "Are you trying to commit suicide? Why do you want to go to Vietnam?" "The army needs me," he said. "They need experienced men like me." We couldn't believe our ears. Before we knew it, he was on a plane heading to 'Nam. He sent us

Polaroid pictures of himself. He looked sweaty in his green fatigues and helmet; he was surrounded by tall stacks of sandbags. We could see foreign words in the background. In another photo, he sat behind a desk on a phone. Behind him was a wall covered with papers held together by clipboards. On the back of the photos, he wrote, "Vietnam, 30 June 1968."

In his passionate letters from Vietnam, he said how much he missed us and that he was determined to buy us a home. Within a year he arrived safely and we were glad to leave Bridgeport. We moved to Goddard Drive in Nahant, Massachusetts, which was near Lynn. We liked living in the military houses there. Unlike Wakefield, the whites in Nahant were friendly and made us feel comfortable. Behind our house was a golf course, and a few yards away we could see the vast blue ocean. Later, the Red Sox player Tony Conigliaro opened a nightclub nearby. On weekends, we enjoyed going to Nahant's beach and taking long walks under the bright golden sun. We were pleased that our father was in good spirits again; he was in military heaven. We listened to his war stories about how Vietcong children would walk up to him looking innocent and how they carried bombs or hand grenades. Or he'd tell us how a young recruit lost his mind after witnessing bodies being blown up into pieces.

By this time, our lives seemed to be back to normal; my father didn't drink as much. I was now a teenager in high school, and he still didn't have much to say to me or to my older brother. My sister was now away in college, and we only saw her during her semester breaks. We noticed that my father seemed to be more quiet than he was in the past. On weekends he would stay in the dining room with the door locked, listening to the radio for ten hours. How could anyone stay in one room that long without coming out? we thought. We turned the doorknob and knocked. He wouldn't respond. Then while we were in the living room doing our homework, he would come out looking distraught. "I gonna shoot him. I'm gonna shoot that son of a gun. Where is my gun?" At first we thought is was a joke. But my father had a serious look on his face; he started searching frantically for a gun that didn't exist. My mother would calm him down and tell him to get some rest. After a while this began to happen more often. Suppose he does have a gun. We were petrified that we wouldn't wake up alive. I was afraid to go to the bathroom in the middle of the night out of fear that he would think I was a Vietcong. At night, we couldn't sleep. During the day, we hated coming home. We stayed out as long as we could. We didn't want to come home to my father's Vietnam.

Eventually our home became a combat zone. His strange behavior grew worse. He didn't want us to make any noise. We had to keep the television volume low. He began to drink two packs of Budweiser a day. My parents argued throughout the night. Finally, they decided to separate. We were relieved; we didn't want to see him again. Ever. He had caused us too much misery. My father moved to Georgia and stayed with his elderly mother.

After ten years had passed, I began to have some sympathy for my father. I now had mellowed and had a better understanding of the plight of veterans, post-traumatic stress, Agent Orange, and how my father had tried his best to keep our family together. I wrote a long letter to him, simply letting him know that it had taken me ten years to realize he'd endured unusual pain and had made many sacrifices for us. He had kept us together as long as he possibly could. He didn't respond, but one of my aunts called me and said that he was the proudest soul. "He read your letter out loud to us over and over," she said. "I told you that my kids didn't forgit me," he said. A few years later, I visited him in Rupert, Georgia. His hair was all gray, and his face was dotted with moles. He greeted me warmly and asked about the family. But still, we didn't have much of a conversation. He pretended that he was too busy to talk, because he was repairing the roof on his sister's house.

I didn't stay in contact with him after the reunion. But about eight years later, I received a letter from my aunt; my father was dying of bone cancer. My husband and I flew down to Rupert to see him for the last time. He was so skinny that he looked as though he weighed a hundred pounds. He could barely stand. We began to talk. As we drank our coffee at the kitchen table, we talked about General Colin Powell; we were both proud of him. Then my father told me about how much pain he was in. He couldn't stand up for more than a minute. He told me that he hated going to hospitals because he didn't believe in medicine. With sympathy, I looked at my father who was carrying on a sincere two-way conversation with me for the first time. Then he grabbed my hand for the last time. "Everybody's scared that I'm gonna die," he said. "I'm gonna live until I get a hundred. Old soldiers never die."

Two months later he died. It was June first. I went to his funeral in Rupert, Georgia. No one else in my immediate family wanted to come. The chapel was filled with my aunts, uncles, neighbors, and his army friends. Young women with their children stood in the doorway wearing hats, fanning themselves in the June heat. Some stood near the walls carrying pink flowers or plates of food wrapped in aluminum foil. As I looked around, I was amazed that my father knew so many people. A group of young army soldiers sat across from the casket where my father lay. A flag was draped around him. As I sat on the front pew, my father's black army friends came by. Some of them remembered me from when I was a child. They had served with him either in World War II, Korea, or Vietnam. I was touched that they had traveled from different parts of the country to be there. When they gave their testimonies, they talked about how he had helped them on the battlefield. They talked about how much they valued his friendship. "He was a rare friend," they said. A lump formed in my throat.

When we arrived at the cemetery, I listened intently to the Reverend. There was silence. I then heard the sorrowful sound of a bugle. The army was playing "Taps" for my father. It almost seemed as though the sound was coming from the vast blue sky. Then two army soldiers began the ritual of folding the flag in slow motion. I watched their hands, their feet. They moved together to the same beat. A young caramel-colored soldier with a mustache gave me the flag— my father's flag.

Although it's been a few years since my father passed away, I often think of him whenever I see Old Glory blowing in the wind. Or whenever I see a lone black soldier sitting on a train. I'll gaze at his green army uniform and then at his cap. An image of my father appears before me. He's young, brown, and handsome. He stands tall and sings the "Star-Spangled Banner" in his tenor voice. I can smell the Vitalis in his hair. I begin to think about the memories—the sweet, the sad, and the painful ones. I think about the days when we were once a family—a military family.

Lise Funderburg

Letter from Monticello

As I drive east along Georgia's Route 16, heading toward my father's hometown of Monticello, kudzu druids loom at the highway's edge. My rental car windshield frames tin roofs, baled hay, and unpaved red clay roads. At the Piggly Wiggly in Jackson, I bear left, cross the railroad tracks, and start looking for the Ocmulgee River, my next landmark. An Atlanta radio station plays a slow piano concerto. Its melancholy fills the car and mixes with the air-conditioning, a breathy, languorous soundtrack.

I have been coming to Monticello since childhood, but never for long or on my own. Usually I travel under my father's wing, flanked by my two sisters, and carried along by the reputation of my grandfather, a country doctor who also became a farmer (perhaps, my father speculates, because so many patients paid with livestock). And even though my father and his four siblings were raised in Monticello, and my grandfather (who passed in 1987) is still considered one of the town's upstanding citizens, I feel like a stranger here.

On this maiden solo visit, I have to lean in to understand the editor of the town newspaper, ask my uncle to repeat himself, and count on context and body language with my father's friend Bubba. They all lean in toward me, too, my angled Northern speech a series of jerks and abrupt turns. Beyond what they say, though, I often wonder what they mean. A person's race, for example, never actually has to be mentioned to be understood. Is it a tonal shift I can't pick up? The consequence of a shared geography and history, common to Southern towns with populations numbering fewer than 3,000? Say a family name (the white Bentons, Kellys, Jordans; the black Tinsleys, Johnsons, Funderburgs) and it bespeaks generations of widely known relationships and economies, kindnesses and cruelties, nearness and distance all coinciding with an ease that I—from a big Northern city, from a Civil Rights Movement childhood, and with a full set of white relatives (starting with my mother)—can't easily translate. In Monticello, the Ku Klux Klan is not some abstract threat. It is an uncle here, a cousin there. As a child, I loved secret languages: But where is the decoder ring now?

I also don't fully understand—but have come in search of— what pulls so deeply in my father, what prompted him to buy this farm after he retired in 1985, to spend autumns on it, and to sneak in weekends whenever he can although, like me, he lives in Philadelphia. Fifty years after moving away from his hometown, he can't spend enough time here. I'm not absolutely certain, but my theory is that although he is one of those men who retired with a vengeance after long years of relentless toil, working the land is the only job he's ever truly desired—and possibly still does.

My father, George Funderburg, spent most of his life as a working man. At ten, he packed peaches. Now those orchards are gone, replaced with pine forests, cattle pastures, and, increasingly, defunct farms broken down into five-acre tracts for new homes (which, in just the last five years, have exceeded all the new housing construction of the last four decades). My father's parents sent him to Atlanta at fifteen for a better education than he could get at the colored school—so second-rate that even its walls were castoffs, built from the detritus of the demolished white high school. During his subsequent and brief tenure as a Morehouse College student ("I was asked to leave," he'll say now, "on invitation of the dean"), he waited tables in a Chinese restaurant and worked a dry cleaning concession. He went on to mop floors at his uncle's café in Alabama and had a short-lived career as a poultryman during World War II. ("It was a failure," he remembers. "I knew how to feed and water chickens, but not how to make them grow. Also," he says, with gasping laughter rising up that eventually will render him breathless and speechless, "people started stealing them.")

Over the next few years, he waited tables on cruise ships sailing between Detroit and Cleveland; sold cookbooks and storm windows door-to-door; shortened his Korean War duty by spending nine months on the front lines; harvested tobacco in Connecticut; and finally settled into a prosperous career in real estate, building a company now run by his stepson. He speaks of these jobs with no ardor or nostalgia, just the matter-of-fact reporting of a past that is gladly gone.

Not so with farming. My father, now seventy-four, who's never had a hobby that I know of, can study the county agent's pamphlets endlessly. He built a cattle chute based on one such publication, and its efficiency in holding cows for worming or tagging has prompted visits from the curious and admiring. His childhood friend Alfred Johnson remembers my father calling when he purchased the farm. "Bubba," my father said, using Alfred's nickname. "Bubba," he said, "I bought a pig in a sack." (I have to ask Bubba what that means when he comes to visit me. "It's when you don't know what you've just bought," he explains.)

"Your daddy loves dirt," says Larry Lynch, one of the local

people my father has befriended since his return to Monticello. Lynch, who's white, is a lawyer, but his heart, too, is in the family farm that he and his brother share and that he claims he'll work the rest of his life to support. "Your dad loves farming so much, it's pitiful," Lynch says, with the empathy of a fellow addict.

Seven miles after the Ocmulgee, I turn onto Fellowship Road, which borders my father's farm. The cattle gate is closed, as it should be, and cows loll about the northern pasture. The cows belong to the twins, Albert and Elbert Howard, with whom my dad has struck a deal, bartering farm upkeep for a portion of their rent. Scuppernongs and muscadines are lush and thick with grapes, defying the summer's drought.

Starting tonight, Troy Johnson, Alfred's younger brother, will preside over three days of pick-your-own, a strategy for putting to use fruit that would otherwise rot on the vine. Maybe Troy will earn enough to cover his time, but expectations, as with every venture here, are humble. After all, my father doesn't farm for profit. The goal, and this is fairly tenuous, is to lose as little money as possible.

My father has wanted to be a farmer since he was a boy, and this 126-acre tract of pastures, forest, and pecan grove is part homecoming, part folly, and part social justice laboratory. When he hires people to work on the farm, every transaction is calculated for its impact on both individual and community. The wage he pays for cleaning his fence line of trash is intentionally higher than what bagpackers earn at the new vast supermarket just around the bend. When Dad decided to build a house, he also decided that any party he ever held in it would be integrated, something that still causes a stir. I don't want to shake hands with the known racists; my father invites them to his home. He donated land he inherited in town for the establishment of a city park but made sure the project's backers would be white and black (even though the site is in a still-all-black section of town—a section some white supporters have never driven through).

My father's breaking ground, but it's ground his father worked before him. Frederick Douglas Funderburg came to Monticello in 1922, straight out of Meharry, to take over the practice of the aging colored physician, Dr. Turner. It was meant to be short-term; instead, Granddaddy spent his career here, ministering to black folk throughout the county and his neighbors up on Colored Folks' Hill. He also helped other blacks register to vote, collected funds to build the county's first integrated hospital—its first hospital of any sort—and treated white patients during the 1938 flu epidemic, integrating his practice from that point on. When my grandfather took over the Masons' building for an office, he circumvented Jim Crow by furnishing his office waiting room with identical sets of furniture on each side, down to the flowers in the vases. Wherever the first patient chose to sit each morning determined the pattern for that day.

Not every problem allowed for such a passive solution. My grandmother was forbidden to shop in town, lest she be insulted, forcing Granddaddy—a loyal and proud man—to retaliate or to pack up and leave.

The more time my father spends in Monticello, the more his language changes (or finds its way home). Consequently, my sister Margaret and I have been perfecting our "Honeybaby" imitation. It must be delivered with a Southern accent, no trace of our father's fifty-two years in Philadelphia. The tone is patient but edged with a slight exasperation that comes out in a harumph. We've isolated two interactions that prompt its use. The first is asking farming questions that are to him too obvious to imagine. Will a cow come if called by name? "Honeybaby, maybe if it's the only cow in the field." The second prompt is suggesting some project around the farm that would demand his manual labor. "Honeybaby, I'm too old to work that hard."

Indeed, my father farms primarily by phone. His hands are big but soft, not like Bubba's. Bubba, now seventy-nine, stayed in Monticello and married his high school sweetheart, a beautiful and sharp-minded woman named Bertha Kate. For the first few years of the farm, before Bubba's health declined some, he was the overseer, something that, in their day, black men never were and something Dad was sure to have painted on the sign at the farm's entrance. Alfred Johnson, Overseer. Dad would call Bubba from Philadelphia with some idea—building a pond or baling hay—and ask Bubba to implement it, setting up a bank account so he could be the one to write checks when the work was done. "We had a good time," Bubba says to me now from across the farmhouse kitchen table. "A good time." I understand what he's saying. I understand, and it fills and it breaks my heart.

Trent Masiki

A Curious Absence

Two days before Christmas of 1997, my father was found dead in his living room, his body bloated and decaying. My mother and I got the news of his death on Christmas Eve, around midnight. We were sitting, when the phone rang, at the kitchen table, talking with my younger half-sister and brother, Kalisa and Joseph, about my going to Trinidad. My flight was scheduled to leave at eight o'clock Christmas morning; I had come to Louisiana a few days before to spend extra time with my family. It was my sister, Jamila, at the other end of the phone. She had been the one most recently in contact with our father, who—like the two of us—was living in Texas at the time.

Our folks split up when we were small. Jamila was three, so I must have been about six. My father made the most minuscule effort to keep in contact with us after he and my mother broke up. He left us in Shreveport and moved to Dallas, where he kept his address and telephone number tightly guarded. He called a few times over the years, but Jamila and I treated him coldly. We were angry because he never called for things like birthdays or graduations. He and my mother were separated for over twenty years, and in that span Jamila and I had him visit us no more than four times.

Growing up, Jamila and I often used humor to mask the pain of being fatherless. We joked about our father being a spy for his home country, Uganda. We imagined that he was in Dallas on a secret mission and that his absence was necessary for our safety. On other occasions, Jamila would altogether deny that we had the same father: "*Kitaka* may be your father," she'd say, joking with me and the family, "but he's definitely not mine." Tongue in cheek, she would insist she was born of an immaculate conception. She was too precious to be fathered by a mortal man. Like Topsy in *Uncle Tom's Cabin*, she sort of just grew.

The disintegration of our family pained us both, but I've always thought that Jamila's suffering was more heartfelt. She was a real daddy's girl. One of her earliest recollections is of our father's Cheshire cat smile. He was crazy about her and she about him. I'm wary of romanticizing their relationship, but they truly shared a bond of unspeakable affection. She was only three when he left, but having such an intimate father/daughter connection severed, even at that young age, was devastating for her. Perhaps she would have better understood why things had to unfold as they did if she had retained memories of the fights and arguments that led to him leaving. To recall those squabbles, to know them from memory as I did, might have made his leaving feel less arbitrary, less cruel. Even though I wasn't as fond of my father, I took the separation hard, too. But my pain was of a different sort, or at least I imagine it to be. I was relieved that the tension in the household would ease, but I grew to resent being fatherless. Although I would come to have plenty of friends in the same situation, it didn't make my sense of being abandoned any easier to deal with.

I'm not sure what compelled Jamila to reach out to our father that September in 1997 before he died. Maybe she was feeling like I'd felt in the summer of 1989. That was when my interest in Ugandan culture trumped my indifference for my father. I was still angry with him, but I had to reach out. I wanted to learn about his culture from him. I couldn't learn it from my mother. She was born and raised in Louisiana; she was African-American. She didn't know Uganda like my father knew Uganda. And I didn't want to learn about the culture from books. I wanted to learn about it from the source. I wasn't totally ignorant of my heritage, though. I knew that I belonged to the Buganda tribe, the largest and supposedly best educated tribe in Uganda, and that I also belonged to the Mamba clan, one of the six founding houses of the Buganda Kingdom. And my subclan, I recently learned, is the Abakerekere, the clan that crowns kings. I have only recently learned this information about the Abakerekere, but this was the kind of cultural connection I was searching for that summer. I needed to have it. I needed to know about Ugandan culture for myself and for the children to whom I might some day pass the name Masiki. Jamila and I grew up in that name, and it molded us. We knew we were Ugandan, and we were, and are, proud of it. We're proud of our mother's heritage as well. But ethnically, we are not full-blooded African-Americans—our link to the Motherland is much too direct to allow us that luxury. Culturally, however, we're quintessential children of the Middle Passage. Our values, norms, and ways of being are distinctly African-American. We don't know how to be Ugandan; it's another luxury we were denied.

Reaching out to my father that summer was no easy task. At the time, I didn't know if he was still living in Dallas, or even in the States for that matter. The phone number I had for him was defunct, and the address was too old to be accurate. So I called the Ugandan embassy and asked for help in finding him. I explained my situation. The official I spoke to was sympathetic, but he could not divulge the information I needed. He took my number, though. Within days my father called me, irate about how I had tried to find him. If he weren't so secretive, I told him, I wouldn't have had to call the embassy. It was after this that we started keeping in touch more frequently than we had in the past. He put me in touch with David and Dan, two of my older brothers living in England. They were children from his first marriage. Their mother, Nanono, had come to America in the early sixties with my father, when he was accepted to college.

David was the second child my father and Nanono had in the States; my sister Ruth was the first. In the summer of 1967, Nanono and my father broke up. She left him. She took David and Ruth and returned to Uganda, where Dan and their three other siblings had been left. My mother, Kathleen, had started dating my father in the fall of 1966. She had no idea that he was married, and found out only after Nanono left the country. My mother had me in 1969. Two years later, she and my father got married. I remember being at the wedding. It was by no means extravagant. It was an informal affair that took place at my grandparents' house. There were no brides-maids or groomsmen, no high-tech wedding photographers, no fancy flower arrangements or crepe streamers. There may have been about fifty or so guests and relatives. It was all very simple and quaint.

There's a picture in our family photo album of my parents feeding their wedding cake to each other. They're in the kitchen standing behind the dinner table, which has been pulled away from the wall to let them stand behind the cake for the picture. My father is dressed in a black tuxedo, wearing his hair in a low conservative cut. His mustache is just as tautly clipped. He's short, thin, and as dark as Hershey's darkest chocolate. My mother, nicely plump and honey-brown, is just a little shorter than he. My father's features are angular and confident. He's devilishly handsome, and his smile, like my mother's, is charmed. Her features aren't as sharp as my father's; they're more rounded and inviting. She has a button nose, strong jaw, and dimpled cheeks. In her pink satin dress, she looks more like a bridesmaid than a bride. The dress, handmade, is a short-sleeved affair with a line of white embroidered flowers running just below the bust. Her hair is trussed up in a pink satin bow, her ears and neck are adorned with pearls. She would have made a lovely flower girl.

Over the years, I've often looked at this picture of my parents. It always pulls me back into the emotional atmosphere of that day. I still bear the impression of being there, of being smaller than everyone else, of experiencing everything from the lowest perspective. I remember being excited by the sense of ceremony that filled the air, but I was also elated because I was acquiring a father, my father. Up until then, he had been a virtual stranger to me. After he finished his B.A. in the spring of 1969, he started working on a law degree that he never finished. He stayed in that program for a year, living in Baton Rouge and making infrequent visits to see me and my mother in Shreveport. In August of 1970, he went to Lagos, supposedly to pursue another degree in law. He failed at that, returned to the States, and decided (or was persuaded) to settle down.

Being excited about getting to have a father is one of the few things I remember vividly about the wedding. The fact that I was around to attend it has always seemed like the most peculiar thing about that day. But recently, a conversation with my mother revealed just how deeply in the dark I've been. My parents took their vows on a hot August afternoon. The wedding was supposed to take place at one o'clock, but it didn't get started until three because my father killed a woman, and that held him up.

She was an elderly white woman, the woman my father killed. Had he been a superstitious man, her life might have been spared. Had he been a superstitious man, he would have remained sequestered in his bachelor's quarters, sipping whiskey and observing the custom of not visiting the bride before she's revealed at the altar. But, anxious to see my mother, he left his lodgings early, breaking the taboo and inadvertently taking a life. My father's weapon was a 2000 lb. powder-blue VW Bug. The woman and her companion, another elderly lady, were standing on the curb, shopping bags in hand, headed back to a convalescent home across the street. My father saw both of the women, but he never dreamed that one of them would, of a sudden, hazard a chance at crossing over and step into oncoming traffic. There was nothing my father could have done; the woman shuffled into the path of his VW at the very moment in which she could have no longer been avoided. That's how the story goes. At least, that's how my father told it to my mother. There's nothing to suggest that things happened otherwise. The police came, made their report, and ruled the whole thing an accident. My father was never arrested or charged with anything. The police simply let him go and sent him off to meet his bride.

I don't know the woman's name. It never got passed down. But I'm an industrious fellow, wise to the art of literary research, and I could comb the local newspaper archives to find the article that mentioned her death. I feel like I ought to, but I don't think I will. For now, this is as much as I prefer to know. I'd rather not erode what has already become a less blissful state of ignorance.

That my father killed a woman is not news to me. That it happened on his wedding day is. I wasn't aware of that until now. I'd like to think that it's not the kind of detail I would have forgotten, but I do forget so much. On two separate occasions, my father showed up at college and coincidentally crossed paths with me. Both times, I mistook him for a stranger. He had to tell me that he was my father, and even then it took me a few seconds to realize that he was. That he recognized me still boggles my mind. If I could have forgotten his face, then it's likely that I forgot that his wedding was marked by such a bad omen, which is what my grandmother, Ruby, thought of the accident. She wanted to reschedule the wedding, but my grandfather, the Reverend Frank Morris, was not given to superstition; he insisted that the wedding go on. This is another revelation. It's something I would have never imagined of Grandy, as we affectionately called the honorable old patriarch of the Morris clan.

These revelations make me wonder. I wonder how many of the guests and relatives knew of the accident. I wonder, in the pictures, is it there on their faces? Is it on my father's face? Is it making his punch sour? Is it spoiling the taste of his cake?

Jamila was lucky that her urge to see our father struck her when it did. We drove up to Dallas and met Vonia, a close family friend from home who had recently moved to the Lone Star state. We all got together and met at my father's place. He was living in a government-subsidized apartment for sick and elderly indigents. Jamila was shocked by his state of health and the poverty-stricken condition in which he was living. She knew he was sick with diabetes because in the nineties he'd gotten into the habit of calling either me or my mother after he'd been hospitalized for diabetic shock. But only

I knew, in a firsthand way, the degree to which he was sick. I had visited him about three times after I'd moved to Texas. I knew that his irises had turned a sickly shade of blue, and that he had once passed out on the streets and awoke to thieves lifting his watch and wallet.

Jamila almost cried when she saw how sick he was. He could barely walk. He hadn't been that bad off the last time I saw him, but I wasn't surprised by his degeneration. I knew he was going to die. I was more upset with than sympathetic for him, because he still refused to tell us why, in over thirty years, he had never returned to Uganda. Jamila and I were desperate to know because we planned on one day visiting our relatives there. But our father's reluctance to return home made us more and more skeptical about hazarding the trip ourselves. We were especially wary because his father hadn't taken Nanono and her children into the clan when she returned. Custom dictates that a mother and her children become part of her husband's clan, and live among his people. Jamila and I wondered how likely it was that we'd be accepted if we showed up on our grandfather's doorstep. Perhaps my father never knew that this issue plagued us. I can't recall explicitly voicing the matter, but he was a clever man—it wasn't beyond his capacity to imagine our concerns. Jamila and I knew that his exile in America had something to do with his father and their disagreement over a land title. This was old news; we wanted the gritty particulars. I told him that it wasn't fair to keep the truth hidden from us since he knew, as we did, that he was soon going to die. He wasn't moved. He still refused to talk about it. Like him, the truth about his exile had to remain a mystery, and we had to content ourselves with that.

After that visit in September, Jamila stayed in frequent contact with our father, and was coincidentally the first to receive word of his death. My mother and I were taken by surprise when she called and delivered the news to us. Our emotions were somewhat restrained. The few tears I cried flowed more out of anger than out of loss. Even in death, Kitaka couldn't get things right. He'd screwed up at being a father, and his death was fucking things up for me at a crucial moment in my life. I was supposed to be on my way to Trinidad to meet my girlfriend's family for the first time. I was considering marriage, and this was a trip in which I'd invested a lot of emotion and money. But there I was stuck trying to figure out whether to go to Trinidad or to stay home and bury a man to whom I had no allegiance and who had never shown any to me.

I decided to go to Trinidad, and that meant the business of burying my father had to be addressed as much as possible in the hours before I left. Money. That was the problem. Kitaka, penniless, hadn't made any arrangements for himself. My mother was in dire financial straits, Jamila wasn't in the best of remunerative waters, and my meager income of graduate stipends and school loans barely kept me afloat. We simply couldn't afford to bury him. His body lay in the city morgue, and if no one claimed it, it would be placed in an unmarked grave and lost to history.

After I left for Trinidad, I had no day-by-day idea of what was taking place on this front. I'd conveniently put myself out of the loop, so I didn't know if David and Dan, once they'd been told of Kitaka's death, understood what might happen. I, however, was content with the prospect of letting the city inter our father. I just couldn't bring myself to go into debt burying him. My indifference upset my mother, but neither she nor Jamila could bring themselves to do otherwise.

I have no idea what my father's parents and siblings must have known or assumed about his funeral arrangements. They knew of the death, but no one in our family was ever directly contacted by them. It seems they were content to let affairs in the States handle themselves. Whether they knew it or not, Kitaka was to be buried in an unmarked grave, and that's probably what would have happened if the Ugandan community in Dallas had not stepped in and taken action. They couldn't let one of their own come to such an uncharitable end. Many of them hadn't seen or heard from Kitaka in years, but they made some calls and money came in from around the city and across the country, enough to bury him in a simple casket and host a small reception afterward. The remainder of the money was donated to a Ugandan charity.

When I returned from Trinidad, I was given pictures of the burial. There are no open casket shots; the body was too far gone to be viewed. All of the pictures were taken outside, at the grave site. They show the bleakest of days. The trees are stark and bare, the ground covered with sparse patches of yellowed grass, the sunlight muted by pallid cloud cover. The casket, rectangular and boxy, is a corporate gray. An arrangement of white carnations sits on top of it, and swatches of baby-blue ribbon undulate in and out of the flowers. Other than those carnations, there's nothing at all decorative about it. It looks like a glorified footlocker, the kind of thing you'd pack away in a U-Haul storage space.

My mother is in a number of these funeral pictures. She's sad and tired, and I can tell that her bad knee is bothering her. She'd rather be sitting down than posing. Jamila, Joseph, Kalisa, Vonia—they're all there, in the pictures. They're all there together—a family—supporting each other. I'm the only curious absence that bears explaining.

My friends and relations weren't the only people at the funeral. There were a lot of Ugandans as well. They're in the pictures, too. Explaining my absence to them must have been embarrassing for my mother and sister. I shirked my duty, left them to shoulder a burden that a less spiteful son would have helped them bear. I abandoned my father like he abandoned me. Of course, I had the trip to Trinidad as an alibi, but when I look at the faces of those dutiful Ugandans, I imagine that no excuse could have been good enough. Some of them knew the trifling details of my father's life, and some of them didn't. In the end, the details didn't matter. They spared him a pauper's burial. To know that he was Ugandan was cause enough to show him charity. I wish it could have been cause enough for me.

Marilyn Nelson

My Cleaning Lady

A friend recommended I ask her cleaning lady to do my house, so I'd feel less stressed. I called the number she gave me, and now I have a cleaning lady. The plan is for her to come every two weeks. So far she's been here twice, the first time dusting, vacuuming, polishing, and then scrubbing my kitchen with such thorough ferocity that she lost track of time and stayed an extra two hours. I paid her twenty dollars extra, and lived for the next week with humble awareness of the giant steps backward in spotlessness the kitchen counters, the sink, and the floor take, every time someone in my family makes a meal or grabs a snack. For the first few days I followed behind us with a sponge sprinkled with scouring powder. But slowly I, a perpetual neatnik who keeps the magazines in tidy stacks, took to letting them lie where the kids tossed them. The second time my cleaning lady came, she did a quick once-over of the rooms she'd already scrubbed, then tackled the bathrooms. There are two. She caulked the kids' shower, fixed the broken light fixture in the shower, and dug out the gunk in the ½-inch space between the sink and the backsplash. Later, as I worked at my desk in the study, which shares a bathroom with my bedroom, I could hear her whispering to herself as she scrubbed. All week, I have lived with the realization that it had never, in all my born days, occurred to me to scrub the bathroom scale. It looks twenty years newer.

We live in a university community in New England. A few days before the first time my cleaning lady came, my son teased, "You're going to have a white cleaning lady?" Then, more seriously, he added, "Mom, your ancestors would be proud." In the recesses of my mind I've heard many generations in jubilation: "Thank God A-mighty! One of our chirrens is free at last."

Every day I light a candle on the credenza in my living/dining room, where a framed collection of family photographs has, over the years, become a sort of ancestors' altar. Aunt Rose sits in front of my grandmother (her elder sister) in the Atwood family portrait that was taken when all of my grandmother's siblings converged to bury their mother. Aunt Rose was a housekeeper all her adult life. She fell in love when she was young, and when her parents forbade her to marry, she and George Freeman eloped. They settled in Cleveland. They had one son. George died young. Aunt Rose was tall, slender, beautiful, and as elegant as a movie star, I thought as a child, in flowing silk dresses or winter suits, delicate high-heeled shoes. She wore her hair in a chignon, and always perfume and jewelry. I loved the grace of her yellow-smooth arms at the piano, the dance of her long, manicured fingers, rough from scrubbing. Aunt Rose worked for the Jeliffs, a wealthy liberal couple who were involved in "causes." Among the Jeliffs's causes, as I recall, was Karamu Settlement House and Theatre. Aunt Rose spoke of Mrs. Jeliff as one speaks of a friend.

A generation later my mother's half-sister, Aunt Charlie, was a housekeeper, too. She and her husband, Hubert, lived in Omaha. Charlie and Hubert had landed there after falling in love and running away from a Jewish mafioso nightclub owner, who—the story goes—wanted Charlie. The story goes that Hubert played the trumpet in a jazz band that had a gig at the club, where he'd met Charlie. In Omaha, he was an auto mechanic, but the trumpet was always in the living room. Aunt Charlie's home was quietly tasteful, with a sunny yellow kitchen, a dining room with a mahogany dining room set (Limoges and a silver tea service in the china cabinet), porcelain figurines on the living room mantel, candy in crystal bowls on the end tables, lace antimacassars on the sofa and chairs.

I had not realized, before the advent of my cleaning lady, how intimate a view the cleaning lady has of one's life. My cleaning lady knows I've never cleaned under the stove-top. She knows I've never cleaned behind the toilets. Our one-sided intimacy shows me that, given our nation's socioeconomic racial history, for many generations cleaning ladies were our spies in the white lady's house. They must have seen and overheard things. They must have whispered things under their breath.

As a student volunteer in Chicago in the sixties, working for The Movement, I once had tea with a wealthy white lady in her North Shore apartment. The mother of a white boy who was the friend of a friend of mine, she had invited me because she was curious about her son's friends. Her living room was a larger version of Aunt Charlie's living room, and she, dressed as elegantly as Aunt Rose, in a dark blue silk polka-dotted dress, poured tea from a silver pot like Aunt Charlie's into gold-rimmed cups of a similar pattern. She was a staunch believer in Civil Rights, she said; she so much admired Reverend King's work. She was proud that her son was involved in The Movement, she said. She'd been raised without prejudice, she said. She loved her cleaning lady, she said. When her cleaning lady came, she said, she allowed her to eat her lunch in the dining room, on her good china. Then she started talking about the Japs. You can't trust them, they're dishonest and shifty-eyed, look what they did at Pearl Harbor. I smiled and nodded, accepting more cookies. I could have responded, but what would have been the point? Every sentence she spoke gave me a glimpse into her grungy places.

This sense of futility describes, I think, generations of the silence between black cleaning ladies and the white ladies they worked for. If ever there was a clear-cut definition of "the veil" separating the races, this may be it. One of my white friends told me that one of his friends told him about Bamanisha, the black woman who worked in his Long Island home when he was a child. He said Bamanisha had practically "raised" him and his brother. His mother paid Bamanisha every Friday afternoon, in cash. One Friday his mother had no cash.

"I'm sorry, I forgot to go to the bank this week, Bamanisha," his mother said; "I can't pay you in cash. Would you mind if I write you a check?"

"No, ma'am," answered Bamanisha.

His mother took out her checkbook. Then, "This is really embarrassing, Bamanisha. You've worked for me for fourteen years, and I can't remember your last name! What an awful thing to confess! But how should I make out the check?"

Bamanisha responded, "Make it to Mary Jane Johnson."

The white woman looked up, shocked. "Mary Jane?! But you told me your name was Bamanisha! We've been calling you Bamanisha for years! I distinctly remember: On the first day you came here, you told me your name was Bamanisha."

"No, ma'am," said Bamanisha. "I said my name Mary Jane. But my friends call me by my 'nitials."

I imagine that white woman, thinking how odd Negro people's names can be, and concluding that Bamanisha's mother must have thought she was giving her baby an African-sounding name. I imagine M. J. Johnson, thinking white people always want to call a black woman out of her name, yet not wanting to correct that white woman, even on so important a personal mistake, for fear of losing a good job. Two worlds, one on either side of the veil. Though it probably still exists for many Aframericans, in the small world I live in, such a deep gulf of silent misunderstanding between the races seems to have become rare.

I admit that this small world may not be "the real world." But it is real, and it does exist. In this world, without secrecy, without shame, families embrace across racial lines. In my circle there is a family which is half Pennsylvania Dutch and half Zairean, a family which is half Ugandan and half British, a family which is half Italian-American and half West Indian-British, a family which is half Aframerican and half Scotch-English American. There are white American families with Chinese or Guatemalan or Yugoslav Gypsy children. There is an Irish-Catholic American family who, by helping their adult adopted son find his birth parents, is now part of a large extended black family in the South. There is a white American family, three out of four of whose children are happily married to a member of other races. My own children have relatives who are Orthodox Jews, as well as relatives who are High-Church Episcopalians.

Of course, none of this may matter in the larger circle drawn around our circle, about which Malcolm might have said, "What does a cracker call a Negro with relatives who are Orthodox Jews? —'Nigger.'" Many of these biracial connections are invisible, causing new kinds of misunderstanding.

For years my white then-husband and I lived two houses away from another biracial family. At one point the other family hired some white carpenters to work on their house. As I walked out one day, one of the carpenters called, "What is this, a biracial-family ghetto?" Speechless with fury, I went back into my house, telephoned my neighbor, and told him about this. He said he knew that carpenter was a nice guy, that there must have been a misunderstanding; he promised to get to the bottom of it. The following day he called to tell me that the carpenter's sister was married to a black man, and that the carpenter was very close to his brother-in-law and his black relatives; so close that he had spoken to me as "a brother" speaks to "a sister." Well, who knew?

Brothers and sisters: yes. Siblings and cousins in families who reunite the peoples of the world. Though the postmodern ethos does not recognize such old-fashioned idealism, still, my twenty-six-year-old German nephew grew up with a black American aunt. My ninety-five-year-old German former father-in-law, when my daughter and I visited last year, shook his fingertips, tightly pressed together, toward my daughter, and said sadly, "I came this close to being your grandfather. THIS close!"

What does all of this have to do with my cleaning lady? Well, she's dusting my beautiful "Mammy" salt-and-pepper shakers, the collection of black angels on my bookcases, the framed family photographs on the credenza and on my dresser. She's dusting the framed draft of a letter my father wrote in April, 1945, requesting individual counsel while under arrest by the order of the Commanding Officer of Freeman Field, Indiana, following a sit-in by U.S. Army officers, later known as The Tuskegee Airmen, in the white-only officer's club. She's seen original oil paintings and prints by my friend Deborah Muirhead. She's seen my Mammy antiques, my Black Madonnas, my Sweet Honey in the Rock poster, my portraits of Professor Carver. She's seen my refrigerator, decorated with pictures of Hattie McDaniels and Vivien Leigh; of Duke

Ellington; of Eleanor Roosevelt; of Xena, Warrior Princess; and with newspaper photos of a mod, long-haired young Tony Blair, of Jesse Ventura in his WWF pink feather boa days, and of Al Gore letting off steam by "getting down" the night after George W. Bush was appointed President.

And she's read my refrigerator: "Art is not a mirror held up to reality but a hammer with which to shape it."—Brecht. "Freedom is what you do with what's been done to you."—Sartre. "The road to knowledge begins with the turn of the page."—Chinese fortune cookie. "If we wonder often, the gift of knowledge will come." —Arapaho saying. "Was mich nicht umbringt, macht mich staerker."—Nietzsche. "Écrire est un act d'amour. S'il ne l'est pas, il n'est qu'écriture."—Jean Cocteau. And my daughter's magnetic-poetry poem: "is it a diamond suit / or is it a gilded void."

She hasn't yet cleaned my study. I don't think I want her to: it's hard enough to remake my order after one of my kids has been at the computer in here. I don't think I could stand to have someone else moving things around. (Half the time I reach for the Scotch tape, it's been moved.) But, like Aunt Rose and Aunt Charlie, my cleaning lady has looked beyond the veil. I don't know what she mutters to herself as she cleans my house, but I see that she values cleaning as a job she can do well, a job she enjoys. I see her sense of accomplishment as she does tasks I do once in a while when I get around to them: taking down and washing the ceiling light globes, shaking out the runner (a piece of fabric I bought in Zimbabwe years ago) from under the family portraits, washing the glass of picture frames. She knows that I value her work, too; that it gives me time to work on other things. She knows me with an almost familial intimacy. While I know practically nothing about her.

For too long, American families were allowed only a similarly one-sided intimacy between black and white siblings and cousins. A black family might know who its white progenitor was, and whisper the names of white cousins, while its white relatives hid the connection in shame, and after one or two generations, were able to forget it. Shirlee Taylor Haizlip's memoir, *The Sweeter the Juice*, powerfully tells a story not unfamiliar, I think, to many Aframerican families. A black friend of mine interested in genealogy several years ago wrote a letter to a white attorney whose name she had found in an Alabama telephone book. She told him that someone with his last name had owned some of her ancestors, and she asked whether someone in his family might have some old family records that might have names of their slaves. He wrote back immediately: he didn't have any family records, but he'd copied her letter and sent it to other members of his family. Some time later, my friend received a letter from an elderly white woman in a small town in Alabama. She didn't have any written records, she said, but she believed my friend had located the right family. She asked my friend to call her the next time she went South. My friend did so, and the white lady invited her and her two elderly aunts (retired schoolteachers, one light-skinned, one medium brown) to join her for a picnic. My friend said the picnic was lovely, and that midway through the afternoon the white lady touched her arm and said, "Of course, you know we're all kin."

A few winters ago, my sister and brother and I, and our children, spent New Year's Day at the home of some of our white in-laws. They live in the country, in a sprawling house with two full kitchens, and there's a barn and paddock for their horses. It was a lovely day; we like and enjoy each other. Since it was a special occasion, there was a special-occasion meal.

The main dish was fresh salmon, slathered with butter, rolled in bread crumbs, and baked until it was tan clear through and every bite was so dry it had to be followed by a sip of water or of the cloyingly sweet white wine the hostess poured from an heirloom silver decanter. On the side were a hot-dish consisting of broccoli spears and Ritz crackers and a hot-dish of green beans and Campbell's mushroom soup, with canned fried onions on top. We sat laughing, exchanging stories of our lives and travels. One of the white in-laws told of traveling alone to work as a nurse in a wild cowboy town in Montana. My brother told of the year he spent as music director of Cirque du Soleil in Tokyo, and of a South African man he met in Zimbabwe who told him about playing with rhinos as a boy (you find a large tree, tease the rhino into charging you, then jump behind the tree; the rhino, since rhinos can't change direction after they've started charging, runs head-on into the tree, then walks around for a few minutes, dazed). My sister and sister-in-law talked about their experiences as actors and directors in various theater companies. There was talk about nursing, about raising horses, about family histories. There was delight. There was coffee. Then there was dessert.

The in-laws brought out a plate of six or seven varieties of beautiful home-baked cookies. These were Christmas cookies; they loved to bake; they were famous for their cookies; they baked these every year. They had saved these for this day. There were jelly-filled cookies, cookies soaked in rum, star-shaped decorated cookies, cookies rolled in coconut. We were urged to take one of each; weren't they delicious, we were asked?

I don't know if it is possible, but I believe every ingredient in those cookies was artificial. They were the kind of cookies that, as a cleaning lady in someone else's kitchen, you might have snitched one of as you scrubbed past, tasted, and then hidden in the bottom of the garbage can. They were the kind of cookies about which, as a cleaning lady in someone else's house, you might mumble under your breath: "What do she think she doing, calling herself cooking, when she don't have the first CLUE about taste? Lord, this woman don't know nothing about cooking. That was the sorriest fish I ever tasted. And whoever told her Ritz crackers go with good broccoli? That green bean dish was an insult to Campbell's soup! Uh-uh-uh." Shaking your head as you pushed a damp cloth around the counter, as you polished the cherrywood tables.

It was the kind of meal that is remembered as an intimate family story, which becomes part of the family history. When my family gets together, there's usually someone there who reminds us of the time the Mitchell cousins, playing Cowboys and Indians, tied my brother to a beam in their attic, went downstairs, and forgot him. Or of the time they buckled our cousin Desiree into the seat belt (this was when seat belts were a brand-new concept) of their family's new car, and told her the car would explode if she fiddled with the fastener. Or of the time they went off to play baseball in the park with my brother, and were on the evening news at the front of an open-housing demonstration. Or of the time my mother got bucked off a calf. Or of the time the dog grabbed the Thanksgiving ham off the counter before dinner was served, and took a couple of bites before it was caught. Yes. Our children will someday remember that dinner, those cookies, and the love with which they were prepared and presented, the love—"Yes, thanks, I think I WILL have another"—with which they were devoured.

In his poem "The Darker Brother," Langston Hughes proclaims

that someday the dark relative will sit as an equal member of the white family at the dining room table. In some circles, that's happening. In those circles, the lighter sibling is welcomed to the black table, as well. We know things about each other; we are siblings. We have looked into each others' medicine cabinets, and under each others' bathroom sinks. We have explored each others' refrigerators and pantries. In this mutual intimacy is the future of our families. And that's not idealism: That's fact.

W. Warren Harper

From *I'm Katherine: A Memoir*

The Matriarch

Dear Aunt Edie,

Katti passed away January 27, 1988. Maybe you know all about it and have actually run into each other. I am sure both of you would end up in heaven, but the population may be such that chance meetings are unlikely. We found out that she had colon cancer in 1985 and she had surgery for the third time; the surgeon thought her chances were pretty good. So, in hope of easing my grief, I started to write my memoirs, or should I say my life with Kay. In January 1989 I visited Brooklyn and I drove past 816. The change, in all of Brooklyn, was pretty disheartening, yet in passing through the old neighborhood all of the old memories came back. I can't recall the first time that I met you, but I have vivid memories of my first visit to 816 when I accompanied the girls for an after-church visit.

I had been calling on the Johnson girls for about two months, and I was beginning to lose my shyness. I met Teddy and Leo, and I fit in with their little group quite comfortably. Your name came up many times in conversations; I even met you on one visit to 902, but I wasn't sure that you remembered. Of course that was early on in my association with the girls, but I remember thinking how short you were.

Now here I was being introduced to you in the basement dining room. I was surprised when you asked Katti if we hadn't been introduced before, but your remark sure put me at ease, and Katti said she had forgotten. Since that earlier meeting I had heard so many tales about "Aunt Edie" that I was convinced that earlier introduction must have been to someone else; this small dignified lady could not be the same person. I can remember being overwhelmed, not only by your presence, but by the sight of so much cut glass, and the huge silver coffeepot, and especially by the large silver tray in your place. I hoped I didn't look like a country bumpkin. I enjoyed every moment and I felt good when you said to come back anytime, with the girls. I don't know if I had romantic feelings for Katti when I tried to ask her to go to the movie; but for the first time I found out how important you were to her when I asked what her plans were for the holiday, because I would like to take her to the movies after dinner.

"We always spend Thanksgiving with Aunt Edie," she said, in a kind of sad tone; then she proceeded to tell me how she gorged herself and how she always looked forward to that day, and it was a big family occasion.

I adjusted to that disappointment, and in a very short time I had become committed to the Johnsons for female companionship. I knew that Katti was the one who saw that I met Leo and Teddy, and I knew she was thoughtful, and I'll admit that I looked for some indication as to how she felt about me. You were so good with your nieces, you made them feel comfortable and wanted, so they looked forward to that first respite from church. Do you remember how we would dance and listen to records and Uncle Jack would just sit there and smile? I often wonder if you and Uncle Jack noticed that Katti and I were falling in love; was it obvious?

Katti always talked of the relationship with you and Uncle Jack, how you took them everywhere: to the beach, on picnics, vacations, and to the cemetery—all memorable occasions for her. After listening to her descriptions, I always wished that I had an Aunt Edie, and wondered how much had I missed by not having one. And then you repeated the routine with our children, so you were grandmother to two generations.

It didn't take long for me to recognize that you were the head of the family, oh, not of Dr. Johnson, but of all the others, and I was determined to make a good impression. As my interest in Katti continued to grow, I began to pay more attention to family. I always felt so free with her, like I could tell her anything and she would understand. In time we reached the stage when we talked of you, and the part you played in the family. You were the head of the household when your parents died and you moved to Brooklyn. It became your responsibility to collect rents, manage affairs, to care for the family, and still go to school every day.

Unfortunately, we were never able to clarify the strained relations over the marriage of Katti's parents, or between Dr. Johnson and Uncle Jack. Too bad, we loved all of you.

You won a lot of points from me when you arranged to go on vacation when Katti and I got married and we spent our honeymoon at 816; that was the most considerate gesture that anyone could have made; after that I knew we would get along. We had a happy marriage so I wouldn't say that our best days were spent at 816, but the introduction to married life was a joy and our duplex apartment was the biggest factor.

It is close to Easter and I have spent a day of watching basketball on television, another one of the newfangled inventions that has captured our leisure time. Easter is always a sentimental time for me so it is an occasion for me to look back at times past and review my life. I spent some time rereading old correspondence, and this includes some of yours that Liz had loaned to Michael; yes he is the family historian and in his own way he is as nosy as you were. One of the letters was from a Roy Kaplow, a student of yours, age eleven. It was written in 1954 and he was now a nuclear scientist, graduating from M.I.T. with honors and he was thanking you for being his teacher at an impressionable year of his life. I thought it was a most beautiful letter and I could see how you lived such a satisfying life. I always remember Katti talking of the many times that she was with you, when you would be stopped by grown men and they would call you by name, saying that you had been their teacher. And then they would ask if you remembered them; most of the time you would call them by name.

I felt like an eavesdropper when I read a letter from Uncle Jack to you. It reads as if you two had separated because one of your friends said Uncle Jack was running around.

God is good, and you reconciled; what we would have missed. What a pity that a so-called close friend, for whatever reason, could have ruined an entire family.

I am so grateful that your niece did not believe in having bosom buddies; I became her closest friend as well as her soul mate, and we made a great effort to keep to ourselves. We were even more private when we moved across country. We just went about raising our children and taking care of each other. We must have had some degree of success because we had marvelous kids. I've always given you your share of credit because you were instrumental in raising them. Even today Kath and I will talk about her days with you, and she still feels that you and Uncle Jack were her grandparents. She even remembers her room.

When I talk to my grandchildren about our life in Brooklyn, you are always a central figure. Katti was amazed at how short you were; a five-year separation, when we left for California, and not seeing you for so long, only then did she realize that you were not a giant. Kath had the same feeling. That was a difficult time for us, pulling up stakes and leaving you behind. In a way I could understand your decision to stay and keep contact with your past, but down deep I knew you were wrong. The past was gone and we were all that you had and we did not have a choice. Our kids were the ones who needed the opportunity for a more secure life. Katti left, and her roots to Brooklyn were deeper than yours—she left the house that she was born in, and her mother was a bride in, and Michael was born in. She knew that Brooklyn was the past, and there had to be a better place for us; underneath, she had pioneer blood. It broke her heart to leave you, but she had tremendous strength. You would not have aged so rapidly with us, the children would have kept you young. It broke our hearts to leave you. Enough of this; let's talk of the good times.

The panned chicken on Sundays, Katti always said no one could pan a chicken like Aunt Edie. "You have to use butter, Kay." And how about when you panned four chickens and Michael sneaked all the drumsticks, he sure was a greedy little kid.

And do you remember the time when Jonathan, in his quiet voice, called you a C.S.? You could be so marvelous, all that you said was, "Little boys pick up profanity so quickly." The parents just looked on aghast. But you were so right; he managed to pick up every word in the book.

And will you ever forget our Saturday nights? They were so memorable, we made a great family. I can taste those hot dogs now, the draft beer washing them down. I always feel good about those times. I'm sure they were happy ones for Mama, and I think she was happy that Katti married someone who enjoyed family life.

And how about the buns and hot rolls from Ebinger's on Sunday morning? I would guess that the DeKalb Avenue markets are in the past. All of the trolley cars are gone; most of the streets are one way. I was in downtown Brooklyn recently and it is a wreck, other than the government buildings and offices. The library looks good and is maintained but Eastern Parkway is a mess. Maybe it was the street maintenance that was underway.

Oh! Memories are so marvelous, and I can understand why you could not leave, except, you need someone to share them with, and that was us. Now I write letters, to the ones that I love, hoping that my thoughts will carry over to them, wherever they are.

With love,
Warren

Catskill High School

Ever since Dad took me to see the New York Rens, I dreamed about playing basketball for the high school. I towered over Dad and felt quite grown-up; for the first time I would do my own clothing shopping, with my money and my selection. Knickers that were full cut and worn midway between the ankles and knees were the newest fad. I bought one gray, and one dark brown. I knew I would be sharp and couldn't wait until school started.

I was a little surprised when I saw the inside of the high school. It was no beauty from the outside, but even worse inside. It was much older than either of the elementary schools, but ramshackle or not, high school was a brand-new experience. The two grammar schools were combined; students moved from classroom to classroom according to selected subject, and teachers taught specific courses; we were assigned to a homeroom. The required subjects were four years of English and History, two years of Math and Latin, and one year of Biology and Civics. Physics, Chemistry, French, Solid Geometry, and Trigonometry were electives. Typing and Bookkeeping were offered toward a business certificate. At the end of each school year all New York students were required to take a New York Regents test for each subject, in addition to the class test. Both tests had to be passed in order to graduate. It was common for many to end their education after grammar school.

I took the two years of French because Physics and Geometry required lab work, and I wasn't going to let anything interfere with basketball. I liked school and did pretty well, especially in English, Math, and History. My father's youngest brother was the only one in his family who graduated from high school, so I imagine that I was thought to be some kind of phenom; I was a pretty good student and athlete, popular in school and well-liked by the town. Maybe a gladiator? Nevertheless, I am grateful to Catskill schools for a sound educational background.

The school had no gym, and that was the main reason there was always a drive to build a new high school. It was necessary to walk to the YMCA for Physical Education or basketball practice. It was almost as run-down as the high school. The court was small, with bleachers on both sides and very little space between the backboards and the walls, and a running track circled over the court. The track was used for standees, and the bleachers were for students and faculty. A new court would pay for itself because the town took pride in the team—the Y was packed for all home games. After the game the two ice-cream-and-soda parlors were crowded, and customers would wait until the players came in to discuss the game. It was strictly a man's world except for faculty and students.

Nothing would have benefited Catskill as much as a new school, with a larger gym to attract larger crowds, but economics were against such plans. I had dreamed of playing against big cities, like teams before us who had traveled to Poughkeepsie, Monticello, Kingston, Beacon, and Hudson. Only Monticello had come to Catskill before, and that was as a favor between coaches.

The first year was one of adjustment for me. Classes were a bit larger and there was a little hazing of freshmen, but I got off to a pretty good start. I was somewhat inhibited because every day after school I had to go to my family's restaurant, the Point, until Columbus Day when the boats stopped running. Of course the money came in handy, but it delayed falling into a routine. However, once the Point closed it didn't take long to fall in with a group walking in the same direction.... By the time basketball season started, I was adjusted to high-school life, but disappointed that freshmen could not try out for the team. I saw all of the home games and I had no doubt about making the squad next year. My academics were good, too.

When school closed and the Point opened I told Mother that there would not be enough time for my piano lessons; that it hardly seemed worthwhile because basketball practice would begin right after Armistice Day. There was no argument, so I guess she knew it was a lost cause. The money could be put to better use.

I made the team. Dad told me I was the first colored player to represent the high school.

I didn't say anything. I knew I was colored, but I had never given it any thought. He was the one who told us not to associate with the kids on Hill Street. When I looked in the mirror I looked just like any white kid—maybe better-looking, too—except I was brown. I talked like them, I played with them, I went to their homes just as they came to mine. We even went to the white barbershop. I guess Dad and his brothers had fought enough battles to remind people that they had better not insult one of his kids. And yet, I can't imagine why I never thought of dating one of the girls; unless it was because none of my close friends had girlfriends.

Basketball practice meant that I was excused from the dinner deadline—I couldn't be home before six.... It was a veteran team with six returning seniors and one junior. After several games it was evident that the coach was not interested in giving newcomers any game experience. One sophomore, a brother of a starting guard, and I were the only subs with much playing time, and none of it important. It was a great team, but God help us next year.

I also made the baseball team, playing right field. I was used to playing the infield but would settle for any position. In all probability I was better at baseball, but it was a bigger thrill playing before larger crowds.

Although the town had a baseball team, it was never as popular as the basketball team. Catskill was known as a basketball town. In those days professional basketball was well-known in upstate New York, and the Howitzers played a decent schedule, always managing to hold their own. They had a center, Toby Matthews, who for years was rated one of the all-time centers.

I was anxious to start my junior year and get on with the basketball season. It would be a very green group, but we would be gaining a transfer from New York, and Warren Hughes, the captain of last year's teams, had another year of eligibility because he'd flunked two classes. But only Stan Fried, the transfer, and I had any polish; Warren Hughes took one look and decided not to play. We lost the first six games, including the Alumni game. And then the coach took sick. The principal chose a young teacher, Ray Light, to fill in. Mr. Light had played hig- school ball in a town near Syracuse, and everybody said he had been on the university squad. He did have youth on his side, and he was willing to experiment. In very short order we shrugged off the six losses and began to play as a team. We became a different group. Warren Hughes had a change of heart and talked to Mr. Light, who said he thought such a move might disrupt the team. We had a fair season, and I was elected captain by my teammates. Our thoughts were on next year, with a veteran team and Ray Light as our coach. It was summer of 1933.

There are a few things of the past I would like to note before I close on this school year: wooden pens with a metal nib dipped in a bottle of ink for writing; ice skates made of steel with a clamp to fasten to the front of your shoe and a strap fastened to the back that you wrapped around your ankle—I was in high school when shoe skates were introduced. Baseball gloves were just a little bigger than dress gloves, football helmets were of leather and the same size as knitted hats, boys wore knickers until they were young men, girls wore cotton stockings and high-topped shoes, laced up over the ankle (so did boys, until high school), bicycles were one speed, you might get a fountain pen at high-school age (ballpoints came after the War), no electric clocks, no wrist-watches, kids did not get braces, birth defects were not corrected, there were no beauty parlors, no Kleenex, no Kotex or Pampers. Men shaved with straight razors; barbershops used hand clippers. Men wore detachable starched collars, carried canes, wore straw hats. Women wore silk, chiffon, organdy, cotton, and wool. Furs were for the wealthy.

I was fourteen when the Crash occurred, but my remembrances of it are not of 1929. I was too involved in school, football, and whatever game was in season—fall and winter meant daily chores and no going to the Point to work with Dad. But it was at the Point that I had access to reading material: New York newspapers were full of national news and the effect of the stock market crash. In the summer months I read more newspapers and magazines than anybody in Catskill. For the first time I began to realize just how small and confining a small town could be. Maybe I was lucky that I knew so little of what it meant to be colored; newspapers and magazines rarely mentioned colored people. I never gave it a thought that only whites worked in the banks or stores; colored people were not a part of my life. I never thought about any ban against playing major league baseball—didn't Edsal Walker play for the high-school team and then the town team? My assumption was they were not good enough; Grandpa had taken me to a Giants game, and they were marvelous. It's amazing how you believe what you read—"All the news that's fit to print"—talk about deprivation.

When school commenced I continued to go to the Point after school and then worked until closing time, until the end of the season in October. I was nominated for President of the Student Body Council, which was called the G.O. (General Organization). Usually the most popular boy and/or best athlete was elected, so it was considered quite an honor. Some of the duties were to meet with class officers to discuss their activity agendas, help new students adjust to high-school life, and to address the general assembly every Friday morning. I was elected by a landslide.

Basketball practice started, and Ray Light would be the coach until the new year, when Shephard—the original coach—was expected back. We added a promising sophomore, but all the other transfer students were freshmen. Practices were organized and Light coached us in some fundamentals; we were at least fifty percent better than the year before.

It was right around the holidays when Ray Light called me aside and asked if I had given any thought to going to college. I told him that it was not in my plans, that times were bad and I would have to help my family.

He told me that he had been talking about me to some people at Syracuse University who were interested in recruiting a colored athlete; he had told them that "This kid isn't white and I am not sure what he is, but he's a pretty good ballplayer." The group told Mr. Light that they were looking at another ballplayer from New York City to come as their first colored athlete; we had no idea how it would go. They said that the recruit would have to play two sports, football and basketball, to justify tuition. It would be a difficult situation.

Then Mr. Light asked me if I was an Indian. I laughed and said I had some Indian blood, just as I have white, but no doubt I would be considered colored. He asked me to think about it.

This was also the year that Dad opened another restaurant, on Main Street near Bridge. The property was a storefront with living space in the back. Uncle Bill agreed to be the day cook provided he could have the living space rent-free. I would work behind the counter, after school until eight o'clock, except when there was basketball practice and for night games. On Saturday and Sunday I worked from eight A.M. to seven at night.

I always worked behind the counter and I took care of the cash register. The first Saturday that I worked with Uncle Bill, I noticed that he prepared several breakfast orders, and instead of passing them through the window for me to serve, he served them himself; they left without paying. I waited until things quieted down and he was preparing the lunch menu, when I asked why those customers didn't pay.

"Don't worry about it."

"Does Dad know about it?"

"I'm the boss when your Dad's not here."

Now I kept track of such incidents, until it was evident that it was an ongoing thing. Then I told Dad, with documented details. He fired Bill and put him out of the apartment that very day.

And to think Aunt Cora always bragged about how close the brothers were.

Dad got caught in the middle of the NRA (National Recovery Act) under the New Deal, when so many small eating places failed because they never paid minimum wage; free meals were always an inducement to workers. He had to choose between the Point and the restaurant. He chose the Point.

I have to admit, my first thought was basketball; I couldn't wait for practice to start. I had a great baseball season, but basketball was my first love. Work at the Point was as hard as ever. Mother had taken my place in the cigar stand, but she worked fewer hours; Dad drove her both ways and I picked up the slack. I guess I had been promoted, because I started to close out the cash register and balance the cash receipts. This enabled me to do my good deed for the year: I started a fund for Mother and Dad's vacation; I don't think they ever had a real one. I put some money away every couple of days, changing small bills for larger denominations every once in a while. When the season ended I handed them about two hundred dollars, for new tires and spending money.

Mr. Light kept urging me for an answer on Syracuse. I talked to Dad, and he suggested I talk to Mother. I talked to her about it; I pointed out that I could be the first in the family to go to college. She listened patiently, but then said, "We always thought you would help the family for a few years."

That was the custom of the times. Good sons did not shirk their responsibilities. I tried Dad again; I imagine he conferred with Mother. The consensus was "It's not possible." I had never really thought of a college; I had never thought of a future. And yet their decision stuck in my craw, mostly because I wanted to find out if I was good enough to compete on a higher level. I didn't worry about classes.

Mr. Light seemed disappointed, but he admitted that a small-town boy would be at a disadvantage.

Mr. Shephard, the original coach, returned to the team after the new year. Mr. Light attended the first few practices. We never heard why he really stopped coaching. Gradually we returned to the old ways of more shooting and less passing. We lost the last two games—to Coxsackie for the league championship, and to Saugerties, our traditional rival. And I had had such high hopes.

After the discussion with Mom and Dad, plus the failure of the restaurant at Main and Bridge, I realized that Catskill was not for me. The other seniors talked of graduation and the senior prom. Two of the boys talked of college. Some of the girls talked of marriage. I didn't participate in the prom or any of the parties; I didn't have a girlfriend. Graduation, diploma, high-school hero no more; what was I to do for an encore? Usually the star basketball player would get a job with one of the local businesses or one of the banks.

The town businesses did not have one colored employee.

In Limbo

I stood on a raised platform at the Armory to address my fellow graduating seniors, faculty, families, and friends. It was my last duty as president of the General Organization; it would be forgotten in moments. I received a diploma that would be tucked away with other memorabilia. I was awarded a prize as the foremost colored student in the graduating class. I had never heard of such an award before, or who might have established one; I deposited the check in my savings account.

I would soon be nineteen years old and I had no idea of what I would do with my life. Career planning was not the custom of the times. But it was evident that this would be my last year in Catskill, so I made up my mind to have some fun. My last rash act was the night after Prohibition was lifted, and I joined some friends at an Italian restaurant for dinner, washed down with beer, my first and it was good. Fun to us small-town boys was strolling on Main Street or sitting in front of the Court House joking with girls passing by; sometimes they would join us, or we might follow them home and sit on their porch. None of us had steady girlfriends and I never thought of dating any of them.

It must have been around the end of August when I talked to Dad about going to the City to find a job, and did he think I could stay with Grandma and Grandpa. He said that things were pretty bad and it wouldn't be easy to find work, but he couldn't see why I should not try. Several days later, Mother and Dad suggested that I sign up with the CCC, the Civilian Conservation Corps, a New Deal program for needy young men. I have no idea who told them about it; I hadn't heard of anyone from town joining. They had certainly talked to someone, and made it sound like a worthwhile thing. Dad thought it would be a good way to get through the winter, and I could return for the summer to work at the Point. I said I'd think it over, but if I tried it I would never spend another year in Catskill, no matter what. I guess that deep down I resented that they would make plans for me without talking it over.

I had to say goodbye to Uncle Bill. Of course he and Dad had patched things up over the restaurant fiasco. He opened a hole-in-the-wall gambling place, but his main business was running numbers. He told me I could work with him, but he thought I was too good a kid to hang around Catskill; he wished me luck.

The County Clerk filled me in on some of the details of the CCC: you enlisted for one or two years, and only a written request from family would absolve you of that commitment; you were paid thirty dollars a month, twenty-one sent home and nine to you; you were given a voucher for carfare to Grand Central Station where you would be escorted to a designated armory.

I departed for New York City on an October morning. On arrival I walked toward a man in Army dress. I joined a group of young men waiting for instructions or for arrivals from other trains. Finally, after roll call, we were transported to an armory where we were separated into two groups, white and colored. Lots of talking and laughing and probably lots of apprehension. I was a bit uneasy with so many colored faces. Probably the strangeness of slang and language contributed; but I would answer and converse when spoken to. We rode all night. We must have been on some sort of troop train because if we stopped at a station I never saw anyone get off or on.

I can't remember where we disembarked, other than it was

close to Williamsburg and Yorktown, Virginia. It was a rundown station and the rest rooms were marked white or colored only. We were directed to a waiting truck for transport to our camp, where we were issued clothing, assigned to barracks, and directed to Mess Hall. We were told that indoctrination would follow breakfast. Food was plentiful—take all you want and eat all you take.

After chow we met Captain Carlson, the commander of the camp. He said we should consider ourselves Army in everything, except bearing arms, drilling, and saluting. "We give demerits when you do not observe the rules; they can affect your leave. We expect you to obey all rules or laws of neighboring communities. You men from Northern states better remember that no colored means just that; we have never had any trouble with our boys."

He thanked us and turned the meeting over to his lieutenant: beds must be made, barracks cleaned, areas outside of barracks policed, reveille must be met, lights out when announced, venereal disease leads to discharge, short arm inspection weekly, and we were advised to have footlockers to secure valuables. Work assignments would be restoring the beaches and coastlines around the Williamsburg area, or any other detail assigned to the camp. We were encouraged to use the library, recreation room, basketball courts, and in the spring tryout for the baseball team.

The camp was pretty evenly divided between New Yorkers and Southerners from the deep South; sophisticate and rural background, the only similarity was color. The thought lingers in my mind that the mixture and Southern locale was a deliberate act to humble New Yorkers; long live the sensitivity of our bureaucracy. I am pleased to say we got along very well. I wrote many a letter for some of the poorly educated. A lot of guys made a business of this.

I never thought of such a thing, but I was not so altruistic that I would not join in a package from home or a pack of cigarettes.

I was bombarded with questions of my origin—I was the only one with straight hair and features—so I quickly became the Indian, finally shortened to Indian. There were few dull moments to barrack life; conversation, humor—tales and lies in varied dialects could be hilarious, and yet made it difficult to fall asleep.

Pay day was a horrible time. Card games and craps games all over the place. Loan sharks sitting back waiting for losers. You could even find marijuana, though it was never used in the barracks. Once in a while a fight would break out, but they were generally just flare-ups; a fight in the barracks would bring serious repercussions.

I discovered that the South could be just as cold as the North. We were pretty close to the James River, I think, and the dampness went right to the bones. The work was hard and we complained about shoveling dirt from one pile to the next, but as much as possible the work crews were rotated to different locations along the beach. Actually we were grading the banks along the river. Dump trucks moved the soil from site to site, then we planted erosion-resistant plants and bushes in the cleared areas.

When there was a call for truck drivers, I applied. I was the only applicant from New York; none of the city boys could drive. The new drivers were given instructions by the Captain: "When you drive the work crews to and from work, you are not allowed to enter Williamsburg proper. A designated and alternate route is in the cab of each truck." There was a white camp nearby that restores Williamsburg proper.

I don't know if Williamsburg had a colored section. Newport News was the nearest city with a sizable colored population; we were advised to avoid white sections. I made two trips to Newport News and one trip to Hampton. Some of the Brooklyn boys wanted to see Howard University play Hampton Institute. They wanted to see Willie Wynn, the first of the great colored high-school basketball players. He was All City, along with the nucleus of the St. John's Wonder Five, around 1932–35. They had a great time visiting with Willie after the game. Of course Willie was older than I, but if he was the kind of ballplayer coming out of the city, it was a good thing I joined the CCC. He was by far the best player on Howard's team.

The trips to Newport News and walking excursions to neighboring towns gave me a little exposure to rural Southern life. There was no transportation to the city except by local cab drivers. The cars were run-down—you never knew if it would break down or blow up. You were in bad shape if your taxi wouldn't start and you had to hire another taxi. If we went to a neighborhood store, it was run-down—shacks, really—and New Yorkers would go out of curiosity, or to get some "white lightning" if they were in need of a drink. Southerners were accustomed to them.

Thanksgiving and Christmas were difficult times, away from home for the first time, but the cooks did yeoman duty in preparing all the traditional dishes. These were the occasions when my letter writing favors paid off; the Southern fellahs were overly generous to me. They were more sensitive and inclined to stick together than the New Yorkers. All of the cooks were Southern, and when they heard that I didn't eat liver, I began to get some kind of sandwich after chow; it would be passed to me in the barracks. When I asked about it, whoever delivered it would say that one of the cooks wanted you to have a little something. I couldn't picture a New Yorker giving a damn.

With the coming of spring an order signed by Captain Carlson was posted announcing tryouts for the baseball team. The old-timers said the way to get privileges was to play baseball. The Captain was a rabid fan who watched every practice and attended every game. Time off from work detail was given for tryouts and practice. The team would play nearby colored teams, CCC or semi-pro. After several practice sessions it was evident that Southerners were better ballplayers, but the best were two New Yorkers who played for the Junior Black Yankees, sort of a farm team of the New York Black Yankees, a team in the Negro Leagues. I played a decent second base, but after five or six games of seeing the other infielders, all thoughts of being a class ballplayer evaporated into thin air. And yet when Captain Carlson got the letter requesting my discharge, he called me into his office; he said he liked my "savvy" and leadership, and he would make it worth my while to stay.

I told him that my returning home might be my family's last chance. We shook hands and he wished me well.

It was a good eight months. I never witnessed so much humor or good-natured kidding; anything that was mentioned could become a joke or a long drawn-out story; almost everyone was ready to share. The idea of separate drinking fountains and rest rooms will always gall me, but if I had it to do over and I had a choice I would choose an all-colored camp. I wonder if any good would come from a handful of whites attending an all-colored camp. Would it solve anything?

Mother

Dear Mother,

The thing I remember the most about my moving to Brooklyn in 1935 was the thought that I had reached the end of an era. I certainly didn't feel this way when I left for the CCC because I knew that I would return for the summer. No, this time there would be no turning back, there was no future for me in Catskill.

Catskill was a great place to grow up. I loved the freedom and the slow pace of the town. I remember the good family life, the good neighbors and playmates. I wonder why I remember so little about Charley, other than going to school with him. Of course the incident at St. Pat's is really etched in my memory, and I guess because Charley was certain we would get another whipping when we got home. Later on I realized how much nerve you had by standing up to that sister and just withdrawing us from St. Pat's.

It's funny how easily children are influenced by adult talk. I remember disliking the Sunday visit with Grandma Harper; she never did anything to me, and she always gave us candy, but I remember the Saturday night gathering conversations about her. Of course I was eavesdropping, but it made me afraid of her. She at least talked with us, even if it was about being good Catholics and going to church, which was more than I got from Grandma Alexander. That could be one of the reasons I hated church.

Katti had a saying: "Beauty can be a curse because others will envy that beauty and try to destroy it, rather than sit back and enjoy looking at it." She was right.

So you started life with a sister who was jealous of you. Why should she, who was four years older, have to be replaced by a sister who was prettier, and adored by her father? A mother who probably had great plans to see you make a good marriage. You will never convince me that she didn't wish for a better marriage for herself. Why else would she be over thirty when she got married, and in 1879 when you know all girls married young.

You graduated from Girl's High, probably the first in your family, and you fell in love with this country boy who was older and worldly, and who knows what else.

Your father—well, he just loved you, the apple of his eyes.

But I'm getting ahead of myself. It is too bad that kids grow up and rarely get to know their fathers; the mother is, or was, the one at home to nurture and care for the children, the father was seen at dinnertime. Just stop and think of it, even my letters were addressed to you. I was a man before I realized what a great father I had. But I do realize that it was no one person's fault, it was the times and the struggle of living. How old was Dad when he finally worked an eight-hour day? You, more than anyone else, knew him for what he was: truly a gentle man, yet courageous in trying times. After all, you were the only spouse who was spared the wrath of Grandma Harper. It's strange how kids pick up likes and dislikes. I liked both of my grandfathers and didn't care much for either grandmother. Grandma Harper yelled too much for me, and Grandma Alexander was too cold and indifferent. I used to like the summer days when Grandpa would sit on the porch talking about himself and then he would question me about myself. On occasion he would talk about spending his last years in the country because he wouldn't have to wait for his vacation to see you. After that I paid more attention to adult talks, but most of the talk must have been private and kept from the kids.

Grandpa Harper never talked about his early life, but every once in a while he would talk about his children when they were growing up, especially some of the escapades that they went through while attending Catholic school—then he would name some of the Irish kids who were involved—many of them were still in Catskill. He said he taught his boys to box, but if the odds were against them they should resort to anything to make things even. He even thought it was funny the way you transferred us to public school, and he would remind me not to tell Grandma. He always found time to talk to us.

I think the greatest change in my life was when I started working in the cigar stand, selling cigars, cigarettes, newspapers, and magazines. That was where I became an avid reader; I read everything: *The New York Times, The Herald-Tribune, The Daily News,* and *The Daily Mirror* every morning, and *The Journal* and *World Telegram* every afternoon. I even read *The Graphic,* the original scandal sheet. And then I read every magazine—*Liberty, Collier's, Saturday Evening Post,* every sports magazine and financial magazine. It was here that I became fascinated with the stock market, and where I recognized that there were a lot of hazards for the ill-informed. I knew it was a full-time job so I never got around to playing the market until I retired. I also read about what your assets should be before you purchased a house, and what your expected income should be in comparison to the size mortgage that you could handle. If I had been privy to your plans, would you have listened to my comments?

When I look back on my youth I wonder if being the older child had anything to do with my feelings toward families; or was I more perceptive. I can't remember ever feeling close to any of them, other than Wini (the only girl), and Joe when he came along, and both grandfathers. It's funny but when I told Katti about Grandma Harper beating up her daughters-in-law, she laughed like a loon, but she understood perfectly: "Warren, your mother is just the same except she doesn't beat anyone up."

It was many years later when she said, "She would like to beat the hell out of her sons' wives, after she put all of her energy and life into them and these women come along and don't even know how to love, cherish, and take care of them." And then she would add, "That's why I take such good care of you, and that's why I would never hurt you; what would your Mother think of me?"

She also told me that I didn't realize how much Dad loved me and how proud he was of me. And how he grieved for Charley, his firstborn. She also said that when I came along, he put all of his energy into me because I looked like you. So you see, from the very beginning, she was sensitive and caring, and I knew just what I was getting.

Strange how I can remember so much about the house on Koeppel Avenue but I do not remember moving there. I do know that I spent my high-school years there and they were happy times. They should have been the best. I was a good student and a fine athlete, popular and well-liked. But home life was changing, and though there was little talk, the tension of hard times was evident to me. Maybe because I was the oldest, I remembered Bushnell Avenue more; that was always home to me. I can remember the kids on Bushnell Avenue asking why did you move? And Billy White saying that he would have gone out for the basketball team if I hadn't moved. He said it was like his brother moving away and leaving him.

It's a good thing that we had simple tastes because there was not a thing to do in Catskill. One movie house, with a change of bill once a week, the high-school basketball game and the semi-pro basketball game at the armory. Our recreation was sitting out in front of the courthouse or strolling up and down Main Street. Ignorance is bliss, so I imagine that is how we survived. Years.

I left for the CCC, and then for Brooklyn, where I met Katti. How can I have any regrets?

Catskill was a great experience, and I have you to thank for it. With love and appreciation,

> Your son,
> Warren

Tara Betts

Peace Offerings

"I wish you were down here teaching," my father says, and then there's this pause. His voice arrives much softer and hesitant than it used to be. I hear the echoes of the familiar boom in his voice from when he whupped me with his big leather belt, or yelled at me for forgetting to bring the salt from the kitchen.

Now, I hear that voice sometimes on my own lips when I cuss out the boy on the train who called me a bitch, or even when I read a poem onstage. My writing is one reason why my father wants me to come home, boomerang back to my birthplace. I silently hope I don't hit anybody in the throat if I ever do.

"I tell all my friends that you teach and that you're a writer," my father has said to me many times. The last time he said it, we were sitting in front of my mother's house, in one of a series of banged-up used cars that my father adopts, manages to resuscitate, and often abandons. This latest one is a station wagon. The fabric lining the roof is long gone; there's nothing there but orange, pockmarked foam. He's wearing one of those green Army surplus store jackets that I used to flop around in as a little girl, when I thought he'd always let me wear his coat. He touches together the backs of his fingernails—from right hand to left—as they rest on the steering wheel. In his momentary lapse of quiet, he looks almost like he's praying with his head down. My father's Afro puffs out from underneath his baseball cap, but that's nothing new. I think silently that he's why my brother Mo and I don't care that much about clothes. What is new for me is nursing his pride and his love for me in these moments too brief. The anger is old.

I think of all the times that I wished he had been there, but my understanding of my parents' relationship has always been different from how my brothers perceive it. I missed every ride on his shoulders, going fishing, the times he dunked me in the Kankakee River—only to jump in after me to start throwing runny clods of mud at me. My brothers were seven and four years old when we left, and too young to remember. They remember his screaming at my mother to "get out and take the goddamned kids with you." My parents fought each other long enough; at thirteen years old, I understood this. Without tears, I started packing my clothes, books, and toys into old liquor boxes from my grandparents' tavern below our apartment. I only cried later.

His anger wasn't there every day, but then neither was he. I hoped he wanted to be there, and cringed whenever I went to the house to ask him for anything—money for a new dress, new shoes, a field trip, a dance. "What do you need all that money for?" he'd bellow, so loud that I would jump. He usually gave us whatever my brothers and I asked for, but we always dreaded the asking.

Now, hearing my father talk, the edges of his voice have softened with diabetes, age, a stroke. So I've reached out to him. I call him, go to see him when I feel brave enough (not often enough), even though I've always been angry about his scant presence in my life ever since he and Mom got divorced. I have always wished for the phone call where he says, "I'm sorry. I should have shown you how loving a man can be." That phone call has never come.

But I had called him at the hospital and made plans to see him this weekend. Then, he tells me that he wishes I was teaching down there in Kankakee. The silence between the end of this sentence and the next one is filled with "so you can be closer to me." It's left unsaid. I hear this silent token that he passes to me, then moves away from by talking about how the schools are different in Kankakee, and how my brothers are asking him for money.

He would never understand what his slightly shaky script on the slim white envelope did for me one Wednesday night. I don't know if it was the passing full moon that marked the end of my period, or the teenager I fired for talking so flippantly about rape—then calling me a bitch for firing her from an arts program, but when I opened the door in the middle of my courtyard apartment building, moved toward the row of mailboxes, and opened mine to find his handwriting on that white envelope, I dreaded reading what was inside; I hurried past it to see what else had come—credit card applications; postcards for exhibits and performances; fliers for my upcoming reading in Hyde Park. That white envelope, with Bennie H. Betts, Jr. scrawled along it, was the only one that mattered.

My father still lived at the same address where I got all my issues of *Teen Magazine*, which had me convinced that I was already too big with too wide a nose and a need for braces at age twelve. The same address where I taped magazine cutouts of Prince on the powder-blue wall since I had the top bunk next to the ceiling. My brothers shared the bottom bunk. I used to imagine my room was surrounded by sky and the blue/white linoleum was a series of smooth, flat stones.

I always loved the way my parents signed their names when I was little. They both used the end of the *s* to cross over the double *t*'s. My mother's is more complicated, like my signature now, but my father made it a clean sweep just brushing the outermost point on the top of the *s* and leaving room for an invisible third line to make a sharp triangle on top of the three letters: *t-t-s*. His capital *B*'s for Bennie and Betts never close on the bottom. Instead they look like the number 3 with a straight-up gangsta lean and the top curve of the 3 slides down to the line where his name rests. The address and his handwriting idiosyncrasies confirm that it's him. It's been fourteen years since we've lived in the same house, and he's never sent me a letter or a birthday card before.

I drag myself upstairs to my studio apartment, fumble with the keys and drop my book bag on the hardwood floor, throw my jacket on the broke-down black recliner, and go to the bathroom with the stack of mail. Put the lid down on the toilet so I can tear the credit card applications in half and throw them in the wastebasket next to the toilet. I won't hear my neighbors talking while I open my mail, and the only other room in my studio apartment where a wastebasket sits is the kitchen. The shaggy, black cover on the toilet lid is way more comfortable. I'm glad I sat there when I opened his letter. Blue lines of a sheet of wide-ruled loose-leaf paper said everything I could have hoped for:

Tara,

I'm feeling better and I loved the card.

You are my love, my joy, my pride.

Look up to you. The way you try to help the young people through your teaching. I guess I'm getting old, went to church last Sunday, we had a good service.

If God lets me live out the rest of my days, I'm going to get closer with you and the boys.

You have grown into a good woman.

Now that the boys and I have bonded into Three Men, I think our love will grow more and more. I will put my heart into making me and the boys better men.

Love your Father,

Bennie H. Betts, Jr.

I immediately started crying so hard that I couldn't tell if it was all the drama from earlier in the day and the disbelief of even seeing this letter, the happiness of getting the letter, or just relief, feeling like I was right all along that my father loves me. I told myself for a long time that people don't love you the way you want to be loved or even the way you need to be loved. It reminds me of a haiku poem an older poet friend, Kent Foreman, shared with me: "She wants me to love / her the way I would love her / if she were me." I've said I wouldn't let anybody hurt my feelings, even if it meant hurting them first. I remember refusing to call my father or send him any cards for an entire year because he didn't go to my high-school graduation. I know now that pushing him away has made me push away any man who might be on some bullshit if he makes me think he doesn't care. Unfortunately, it's been more than I care to claim, and some men have done so much to redeem their gender in my eyes. Most of the writers that know me are quick to say that I threaten people at poetry readings, and have dubbed me as Bennie's child for real—"Ruffneck Rita," aka Ms. Section Eight 1987.

One of those writers was the first I called after reading my father's letter, snot on my face. Tears clogged the receiver so densely that he hung up on me twice. He couldn't even hear me until I blew the moisture out of the phone and called a third time. All I had to tell him was my father wrote to me. He said, "It's good to heal finally, isn't it?" Yes was the only word I could say for about five minutes.

I called this friend because only two or three men would have any idea what my father's letter meant to me. He was the only one in this handful who understood personally how my cynicism about men leaked into my writing and exploded in failed relationships, and one with him. He knew times when I would scream at the top of all my organs, cuss, and even throw blows if I thought the man wasn't listening, wasn't being respectful, or was just being shady and trifling.

He described me attacking him once. He said I lunged at his neck with my hands while he stood a few steps below me against a wall on a staircase. On another occasion, if that's what I can call it, he smacked my hand off the knob of the car stereo I had just turned off after telling him that I wanted to talk to him. Every drop of fury raised my hand and knocked off his glasses.

He never forgot that, and he never loved me the same, just like I never loved the boyfriend who hit me years before, just like my momma never loved my daddy the same after he hit her, stayed out late, or picked at the dinners my mother cooked. My mother asked us constantly, "How's the food? How's dinner? Is everything okay?" for almost two years after we left my father's house. It took me a few months to realize that she asked because Dad would always say something about the food like, "That's it?" or "You ain't season this enough." Always saying something. I had to tell her a couple of times, "Mom, you're not cooking for Dad anymore. It's fine. It tastes good." Then she got comfortable with letting the spaghetti stick to the bottom of the pot or baking frozen fish sticks more often. I knew I couldn't be like my mother was then, and I never wanted to lose my temper like my father; but I have.

Be patient and think through all of the alternatives. I keep telling myself that. Luckily, I saved the friendship with the writer instead of fucking it up, although I've been angry in varying degrees, like warm water for washing hands instead of through-the-lid boiling to scald the skin. He and I still talk to each other and we are still trying to heal, but never seeing a relationship work has always nagged me. I wished my father would give me advice, tell me his outlandish stories, visit me—not just for my college graduation, but just to check on me. Standing in the trenches of myself, I would ask, *Why would any man have my back, if Daddy is only around sometimes?* Then all the rationalizations would jump out of my brain: I am a good person. I've done well in school, graduated from high school and college. I've won awards. I try to be nice to people. I'm not at all bad to look at. I'm affectionate. I'm well-read. Is there something wrong with me?

You've got to believe stuck in my head like an old Lenny Kravitz song. So I am waiting to be wrong about desertion, so I can be in the right place with the right person.

My mother doesn't know what having the choice to wait is like. She started seeing my father when she was fourteen. When she was eighteen or nineteen, she had me. She and Dad got married when she was still pregnant with me. I asked once what she had wanted to be when she grew up. She said she couldn't remember. "I had you and the boys and I just never got around to it. I don't remember," she repeated.

My mother forgets things sometimes, but remembers little things, or makes odd observations like, "I always thought Bennie was kind of orange." She said this when we were talking about all the different shades that black folks are. It's strange hearing your white momma talk about the hues of black, but we understood each other, even though I think his undertone is more yellow than orange. It depends on what you see.

By the time my parents separated, my mother was ready to see, and say, that Daddy wasn't shit. "He knocked out some of my teeth. He pushed me down the steps and messed up my knee. He was always yelling at me and you kids. He gets high and fucks up the money. He never wanted to give me enough money to take care of the house. He was always...." Even though it was true, I didn't want to hear it. "Momma, you ain't got to say all that because he's still my dad. He's the only dad I got."

Sometimes she'd stop then, knowing she was within earshot of my little brothers. My brothers didn't need to hear that. Once, the older of them put his head down when she launched into the verbal assault. My mother never let us even hang pictures of him with us in "her" house. Besides, he didn't help her get this house or get one when they were together. I didn't understand until I was grown that she no longer wanted to deal with a relationship gone bad.

I've told my father about confronting my mom when she said these things. While I was in college, I wrote to him once in a while or sent him a card that reminded me of him. Sometimes, I remembered his birthday, or Father's Day. Lately, I've started calling him when I can, even before he had the stroke. I've described to him the highlights of my holidays, like how I watched the Christmas Day 2000 solar eclipse through the glossy, cardboard frames of protective glasses. Writing to him, talking to him, seems less scary now than when I was ten, twelve, or even eighteen years old.

This is a change that I think my mother doesn't understand, because of how he treated her. Every now and then, I mention something that sketches another dimension of my father as a man she never knew. When I had a tumor behind my heart that grew to the size of my heart, my mother visited every day and helped pay for the surgery. She and the boys came with teddy bears, a spotted cow that mooed upon squeezing, and a big Tasmanian Devil pillow shaped like the cartoon character's head. Taz made sleeping bearable, and my mother would often come in and find me sleeping with it. My arms wrapped around Taz as it covered half my head and upper body. He greeted people as they entered my intensive care room when I was too tired to wake up. My mother has and always will be there for me, and she knew how much the white teddy bear with shiny golden wings meant to me. Dad gave it to me during his one visit to the hospital. He pressed on its chest with his huge hand and it said, "I'm your guardian angel. I'm your special friend." I pressed its little white body until its battery-powered voice grew silent. The Catholic schools and prayers have ingrained me with a love for angels, and I loved this one, even though I suspected his girlfriend helped him pick it out.

While I was in college, my father and cousin came to the apartment where I lived with the boyfriend who hit me. My father started talking about how he never approved of me moving in with him in the first place. I didn't want to be blamed for being popped in the head, so I snapped: "You never said anything and you haven't been around! You're supposed to be here to help me, not take his side! You have a lotta nerve after what happened with you and Mom, because you used to hit her!" I yelled at him and saw his head drop, along with his voice. "Your mother and I are another story. . . ." he said, trailing off.

"But it happened," was how I ended it.

He helped me move all my things. My mother sounded surprised when I told her he didn't say much.

Shortly after I turned thirteen, my father dropped me off at the Kankakee Public Library, since I had a paper due for the end of the school year. We drove up to the front of the library in the dark tan Cadillac that we used to have. The air conditioner was going full blast and yet my father still sweated. Then I realized he was crying. "You mother and I have been fighting a lot. I just want you to know...that whatever happens...I love you. I love you kids," he told me. I didn't know that my parents' separation was so close. I told him that I loved him, too, and said goodbye as I walked toward the black metal lions guarding the library's doors. He watched me walk into the open door. When I mentioned this early goodbye to my mother about seven years later, she asked, "He cried?"

Just before his stroke, I found myself sitting in his station wagon. We had just returned from stopping by Grandma's house, then the gas station near Harrison Avenue and Station Street where he worked. He wore his black baseball cap over his Afro, and an Army jacket. He told me again how he tells his friends that I write, that I teach. It felt as though he were proud of me. He was looking into his hand when he said, "I want Grandma and Grandpa to leave you and the boys the house. I don't need it no way." Later that night I told my mother what he'd said. She cut in by saying he probably felt bad about never treating us right in the first place. I said, "Maybe, maybe you're right, Ma."

Before his stroke, I felt like I was edging closer to my father. I am still curious about the paternal side of my family tree, even though I grew up around my paternal grandparents and Uncle L.D. on Evergreen Avenue. I visited distant cousins, and even Great

Grandma Bessie Betts in Jackson, Michigan, a few times. I'm trying to take time slowly, to build my courage, but I think my father's stroke has pushed the hands of his clock to move a little faster. My mother hasn't heard me articulate most of these thoughts as words, spread out on the page like cowrie shells, gathered to be strung around my neck or hung from my ears.

I don't know how to tell my parents how I see them. I don't know how to tell them that I think sexism debilitates women, but also that it cripples men like my father, who were never taught or encouraged to talk to their daughters. How do I say that I hated the way my daddy treated Momma, but that on occasion I wished they had worked it out? How do I make my mother see that I don't like what he's done in the past, yet despite his flaws, my father is not anyone's enemy now? I know I can't make either of them talk to the other, and that's fine with me.

The only thing I can offer my parents is my willingness to talk to them both. I can recognize birthdays, Father's Days, and Christmas in more than one house. I can recall the moments where my father has scratched the surface of himself to offer glimpses of the person my mother never knew. I can offer my mother anecdotes from the pockets of my mind. Fragments where my father calls me sugar lumpkin or sits next to me with unapologetic tears as he tells me he loves me. Moments where he quietly looks down at his hands on the steering wheel. The time he came to my debutante cotillion with what might have been a broken foot after working on a car, just so he could be my limping escort. His hands passing a white angel teddy bear into my hands. His letter that I imagined I'd never receive. His words stating clearly his pride, his love. The only explanations that I can offer my mother, or anyone else, is that my father and I are giving each other something, no matter how small or short-lived it may be. My father and I are making peace offerings to each other, and I'm just now realizing his past offerings, in retrospect.

Edwidge Danticat

The Future in My Arms

I had never held any living thing so tiny in my hands. Six pounds and one ounce, lighter than my smallest dumbbell was my newborn niece, her face bright pink, her eyes tightly shut, her body coiled around itself in a fetal position, still defiantly resisting the world into which she'd just been thrust. I had been awaiting her birth with feverish anticipation; I was going away for the summer, and I didn't want to leave before she was born, only to come back eight weeks later and find that she had grown accustomed to most things in the world except her only auntie on her father's side, the sole woman child in a family of men, who all her life had dreamed of having a sister.

She arrived the day before I was to leave. I was at the Brooklyn Public Library researching an article when I called to check my messages. In a breathless voice, my brother Andre announced, "You are now the proud aunt of Nadira Amahs Danticat. Her name means 'She whom God has chosen.'"

I ran out of the library and headed toward a flower shop on Flatbush Avenue. As I approached, I heard someone call out my name. It was my brother Karl and his partner, Mia, who were expecting their own child in a few months. They, too, were heading to the hospital to see Nadira.

On the way there, I remembered a message that a girlfriend of mine, a new mother, had sent me for my thirtieth birthday a few months before. "May your arms always be a repozwa, a place where a child can rest her head," it said. I had told her that two of my brothers were becoming fathers, and she had wanted me to share those words with them. But I'd decided to wait until both my niece and nephew were born to share this with their parents—that we had each become a *repozwa*, the Haitian Creole terms for "sacred place," in whose shelter children would now seek rest.

By the time we got to the hospital, my sister-in-law, Carol, had already had a few visitors. She appeared exhausted but in good spirits as she and Andre took us down the corridor to the maternity-ward window. Which one was Nadira? Andrew wanted us to guess, to pick her out of the rows of infants like a long-lost relative in a crowd of strangers. We were aided in our task by the small pink name tag glued to her bassinet. Carol asked if we wanted to have a closer look. We went back to the room and waited for the nurse to bring her in.

We all stood up when she was carried in. I knew I was getting ahead of myself, but this made me think of a wedding where everyone immediately—and almost instinctively—rises to greet the bride. She was passed from loving hand to loving hand, but I kept her longer. I would soon have to leave, so I wanted to hold her, to cradle her in my arms, let her tiny head rest in the crook of my elbow. I wanted to watch her ever so slightly open her eyes and tighten her mouth as she battled to make sense of all the new sounds around her, all the laughter, the wild comparisons with relatives living and gone, all so very present in her face. I wanted to read her lines from Sonia Sanchez's "Poem at Thirty": "i am here waiting / remembering that / once as a child / i walked two / miles in my sleep. / did i know / then where i / was going? / traveling. i'm always travel-ing. / i want to tell / you about me . . . / here is my hand."

Nadira's presence had already transformed the room. Her opening her eyes was like a Hollywood press conference, with all the video and picture cameras going off, trying to capture something that perhaps none of us knew how to express, that we had suddenly been allowed a closer view of one of life's great wonders, and by being there, were an extension of a miracle that happened every second of every day in every part of the world, but had generously now granted us a turn.

That day, when we lined up for a glance, a touch, a picture, and tried to imagine a life for Nadira in a new country, we each made our own silent promises not to let her face that new world alone. We were telling her and her parents that we were her village with our offers of baby-sitting favors, our giant teddy bears, our handfuls of flowers, and the crooks of our arms and necks and laps, which we hoped that she would run to if ever she needed a refuge.

Looking back on my own thirty years, having crossed many borders, loved and lost many family and friends, young and old, to time, migrations, illnesses, I couldn't help but worry for Nadira, and for my nephew yet to be born. Are there ahead for them wars, a depression, a holocaust, a new civil-rights struggle as there were for those children born at the dawn of the last century? Will they have to face the colonization of new planets, genetic cloning, new forms of slavery, and other nightmares we have yet to imagine? Will we, their tiny village, give them enough love and assurance to help them survive, thrive, and even want to challenge those things?

Before handing Nadira back to her parents, I felt torn between wanting her to grow up quickly so that her body might match the wits she'd need to face her future and at the same time wanting her to stay small so that she might be easier to shield and carry along the length of our elbows to the reach of our palms. I wanted to tell her parents that though I had never held any living thing so tiny in my hands, I had never held anything so grand either, a bundle so elaborately complex and yet fragile, encompassing both our past and our future.

Though Nadira and my soon-to-arrive nephew were not created specifically with me in mind, I felt as though they were the most magical gifts that could ever have blessed my thirtieth year of life. Humbled by my responsibility to them, I silently promised their parents that for the next thirty years and the thirty after that, my heart and soul would be their children's repozwa, a sacred place where they would always find rest.

[Note: The author's nephew, Karl William Ezekial Danticat, was born on August 23, 1999.]

Karen Chandler

Making Noise

As I lay still on the misshapen mattress in my new apartment in West Philly, I waited for the comforting nighttime sounds of my new neighborhood: the light rumble of a late Spruce Street bus gently shaking the ground under my apartment building, the loud calls of the few remaining cicadas, the closing of car doors, and the jangling of keys. I was finally relaxing, having put to rest, at least for the moment, my questions about whether my recent move and graduate study at Penn were the right choices for me. I had stopped worrying about my aging uncle Quentin, who would die at the end of autumn, my mother's valiant efforts to keep up her house and yard in our old, declining neighborhood in St. Louis, my sister's frustrations with her job as a hospital administrator in Chicago. I was only minutes from sleep, when I heard Eric, the young man whose loud talk regularly awakened me as he ventured home down the side street I lived on. That night I had hoped to fall asleep before he'd found himself near home. Usually, his reporting on his successes or frustrations with dates (whose names varied with the night), and his calls to friends to acknowledge the quality of one of his performances in love or work or competition with a peer, put me in an angry mood that kept me awake far longer than I'd want to be. I wanted silence and sleep, not some high teenager's monologue about his life and loves. Yet my anger also sprang from envy, I think, for somewhere within me I also wanted aspects of this stranger's life—friends, romantic experiences, a power of self-assertion—that eluded me. That night I didn't envy him, though. As he stopped near the stoop under my third-floor window, he yelled out, "I've known loss." He went on to shout, "They killed my daddy. And they killed my brother. They killed my daddy. And they killed my brother. They killed my daddy and they killed my brother." He sobbed loudly for several minutes; then I got the silence, but not the peace, I'd longed for.

Coming home from Penn or Center City after that night, I'd often walk by way of Farrugut, the street down which Eric's voice always disappeared. I wondered if I'd ever see him or hear his voice by day, but I never encountered him. The groups of young black men I passed in the neighborhood were always quiet, playful, and self-contained, with no great anger or sadness spilling out. On dry nights in the following spring, I would occasionally hear Eric's voice as he stopped near the stoop under my window, smoked for a bit, and checked in with friends before going home, but he offered no more desperate disclosures. In the next year, his little sister stopped calling him home for dinner, too, so I gathered he'd left the neighborhood and the city to pursue the things young men do. Yet his mournful, angry call stayed with me. Hearing Eric's pain certainly didn't provide me with any great insight into his condition or lead me to welcome his more routine noise-making, but his piercing words did make me want to hear him again, to create a fuller picture. I never got angry about his loudness again. Instead it became one of the sounds that put me to sleep, for it affirmed his continuing need for attention, it signaled his self-importance, it confirmed the continuity of life in a world in which black men's voices too often fall silent too early.

Eric's cry tapped the fear and anger I had carried ever since I was a child in St. Louis and became conscious of the precariousness of life, particularly the vulnerability of the men in my family and neighborhood. When I was six, I came home from my grandmother's and found my strong, gentle father half-conscious, spread out on the kitchen floor after having had a heart attack. Daddy recovered well, but in the week he was in the hospital, my grandfather and my father's older brother Houston also had to be hospitalized because of illnesses. I don't remember feeling confused or terrified, but I must have been, for these men, along with my mother and grandmother, represented security and comfort for me. At six, I understood the men's troubles as physical. But I gradually came to associate their physical ills with the troubles of the world. My grandfather returned home with an unsound mind, given to calling my grandmother names and blaming her for all he'd lost (that is, his inheritance—crop- and oil-rich land in Kentucky— given up for marrying a dark-skinned woman, fifty years before, against his father's will). My uncle returned to his job as a principal in a school for teens with behavior problems. Daddy returned to his station house, not as a police detective, but as property manager, as organizer of stolen goods. When I was twenty, three years before I'd moved to Philadelphia, he died from another heart attack, and I still ascribe his death to his caring too much about people he couldn't help or who couldn't help themselves adequately, and to his trying to be good in a world that didn't support his efforts. A neighbor, Glen, who has been in and out of jail for thirty years, told my sister Joyce tearfully that "Mr. Chandler cared for me and my friends. When we were in jail, he'd come see us, bring us cigarettes or snacks, never talk down. He loved us and we loved him."

I think this is true; my father certainly was an empathetic man, but his empathy didn't come easily or painlessly. When I was in high school in the late 1970s, I was alone with Daddy one afternoon before he left to pick up my mother from work. He told me how pleased he was that I was persisting with calculus, even though it was often very difficult. Then, he added that he was glad he had daughters. He explained that sons often used their strength to fight each other and to fight themselves. He said they got caught up in destructive competitions that led them nowhere. At his age, he said, he didn't have what was needed to deal with such behavior. I wasn't prepared for this confession because my father tended to avoid generalizations and because the boys I knew, though competitive, didn't seem bent on destroying anyone. My suburban cousins who were closest in age to me were so consumed by music-making that they seemed detached from my world except when I occasionally joined their funk/dance band to play keyboards or sing backup. My male friends from high school competed for girls' attention and for academic honors. They were mostly scholar-athletes whose competitions typically took the form of political, ethical, and aesthetic debates; they showed off their insights about local and national politics, George Clinton's harmonic and rhythmic innovations, Henri Matisse's color and contours, and Mark Twain's racism with equal passion. Even the few who sometimes drank too much or smoked weed too often didn't seem headed for destruction. All were rightly optimistic about their prospects for college and for future careers through which they could assert themselves and exercise their creativity and intellect as lawyers, writers, physicians, engineers, and computer specialists.

Yet I know my father's words were relevant. Though I often hid behind the pages of fat British and Russian novels, I witnessed the alarming disappearance of the young black men from my neighborhood and the increasing precariousness of my older male cousins' lives. Many of my neighbors left nearby high schools only to move on to the liquor store around the corner, where men of various ages negotiated the ways they'd assert themselves in the world. There are Glen and others like him who have managed to hang on. Yet many would go off to jail for possessing weapons or drugs or for stealing cars or televisions, come back home only to return to jail and die there, falling to the murderous rivalries of gangs. My cousins avoided jail, but they've had their share of trouble. One, a cool trickster who'd begun college at sixteen in the 1950s, and another, a high school track star with astonishing good looks, secured jobs with benefits, drove fine cars, and lived in stable neighborhoods, only to become addicted to cocaine and estranged from their wives and kids. To this day they struggle with their addictions and their aging bodies, they struggle to maintain ties to family, and they struggle to rework their images of themselves, their understanding of who they are and what they can be.

The story of how our society threatens to deny or kill young men's spirits is not new. Perhaps that story is not the one to which Eric's cry referred. Yet I can't separate my memory of Eric's cry from my concerns about how our country denies so much to African-American boys, except blame for social problems. A friend recently told me how her adventurous three-year-old son is regularly accused by one of his daycare teachers of mischief that other children perpetrate. Like my friend, I'm concerned about how to protect a young boy from such injustices. We want to raise our sons in ways that foster their particular voices and that give them the confidence to use them. I certainly want my son Benjamin to be able to raise his voice to celebrate life, not just to acknowledge losses.

House Calls

Benjamin, like most three-year-olds, loves to make noise. I've understood his noise-making to be an important means not only of asserting specific needs but also of expressing and sharing his creative spirit. Still a lover of quiet, I try to accept and celebrate most of his noise. I've come to see that his noise-making has made me into a more receptive and creative person. About a year ago, we were having breakfast together, and after wiping grape jelly from his mouth and place mat, he asked me to take his napkin, singing a Rossini-esque recitative, "Here you go. Here you go." He held each of the last three syllables, passed the napkin on, and returned to his meal nonchalantly. At that moment I realized that many of his requests and commands are sung, often in his unbelievably deep baritone, sometimes in a tenor that seems less natural to him. At times he plays up his status as performer, holding his head back or playing his imaginary rhythm guitar, as he sings. Yet often he seems to be singing without much thought of an audience. Though he goes for long stretches not using recitative, he still resorts to it, to emphasize his sense of play and his point. Last week, while he set up train tracks in his bedroom in our home in suburban Louisville, I was cleaning next door in the bathroom. When I'd finished my work and entered his room, he sang out in a staccato baritone, "Take the train, take the train, take the train that's blue. / Not that one, not that one, not that one. Here!" Kneeling before his four-looped track, he bounced to a beat recalling that of a warm-up song at a college football game. I adapted my voice to Benjamin's beat and sang back that I was happy to join him; then he showed me which track to use for my train.

Serving as Benjamin's regular collaborator in call and response, I wonder about his ability to get me to sing to his tunes. A Guatemalan student of my brother-in-law Patt had a possible explanation. When she saw a photo of Benjamin in Patt's office, she stood transfixed for a few moments and remarked, "He has the eyes of a conqueror." Singing with and for Benjamin is a big stretch for me, and he, both in the womb and beside me, has inspired me to sing out loud, which I simply didn't do most of my life. I feared being heard and found wanting as a singer. I might imagine that I was singing to Barbra Streisand's "Quiet Night," Rosetta Tharpe's "Precious Memories," or Cassandra Wilson's "Harvest Moon," but I wouldn't make noise. After I confessed to my husband's cousin that I didn't sing out loud, even around the house, because I wasn't a very good singer and wouldn't want to offend anyone who might hear, she said to me, "Does it really matter? Sing for yourself." I've begun to, for myself and for Benjamin. I don't want him to grow up as concerned as I've been about how the noise I make might affect someone else. I'm finding that I like raising my voice. And now my collaborations extend beyond my play at home with Benjamin. During a recent trip to Chicago, Benjamin and I were driving to the Children's Museum with my older sister Joyce. A song Joyce and I liked came on the radio, and we both joined the singer enthusiastically. From his car seat, Benjamin, not knowing the words, also joined in, by swaying back and forth, gently kicking the seat backs, and smiling.

Being a mother has meant developing my voice and my confidence more; it's meant being more consistent and open about expressing my will. Like Benjamin, I have a strong one and I can exert it. My quiet manner, however, seems to deceive friends, acquaintances, students, and colleagues into thinking that I'm naturally quiescent or weak or excessively shy. In grad school a friend, on reading my prospectus for a filed exam, asked me if my faculty advisor had written it. I was taken aback, and asked what she meant. She responded that the prose was so "commanding" that she didn't see how it could be mine. More recently, a colleague, who had visited one of my classes at the University of Louisville where I teach, expressed surprise that I could be heard above a whisper. Having long been aware that people can have "several voices, as well as two complexions," I find these miscalculations somewhat odd. Of course, they're partly inspired by an image that hides the self-assurance and self-dependence that are as central to my character as my shyness and self-doubt. As a mother, I'm finding that I'm more willing to share those apparently less obvious aspects of self, not primarily to accommodate others but rather to accept and express myself beyond the private realms of my life.

My father, whom Benjamin is named after, taught me the importance of listening to others and expressing myself, but he has also served as a standard that I've believed I've fallen short of. Daddy was a great, entertaining talker who made stories come to life; he was also daring and outspoken, given to asserting what family members, neighbors, and co-workers might not want to hear. As I grew up, I heard my father's voice more than anyone else's. Indeed, I associated his booming voice with home. As Daddy would come inside the house, he'd call, "Karen, Kaaaa-rennn." And I'd answer, "I'm here, Daddy." Often, his call required only that reply and not my attendance or prolonged attention, for he'd often go to his basement workshop or our garden in the backyard, while I'd continue reading a novel in my room or doing homework in the kitchen. Yet our vocal exchange was a welcome refrain that expressed our need for each other, our comfort in each other's proximity. Of course, his voice affirmed that he had survived the dangers of his job and of our neighborhood. After his first heart attack, when his job changed and he took to wearing a uniform, he'd put on civilian clothes before riding the bus home from work through North St. Louis, because a uniform might provoke attacks. For him, my response to his call affirmed that I, too, was still alive. Just as he had survived the threats of a neighbor, Mrs. Cole, that she would kill "that police-uniform-wearing black man" two doors down, I had survived her threat to "do away, so help me God, with that fast little ponytailed girl."

Often Daddy's voice was a prelude for our getting together and for his sharing a story about his co-workers. His most entertaining stories tended to trace the foibles of police officers who had too much confidence and too little sense. Sometimes the stories would end with the foolish officer's comeuppance. The recurring theme was the importance of self-reflection and of carefully observing and listening to one's associates. An implied message in many of the stories was the need to not be passive, to question authority, to not assume that the people with authority should have it. When I was growing up, the irony of my father's teachings escaped me: he was, after all, a representative of law and order, an imposing figure of authority even without his badge and gun. He represented setting high standards, being responsible, and following rules. Yet he also illustrated how personal those goals could be, how detached from other people's expectations.

I am still learning how to apply Daddy's lessons to my life and thinking about how to present them to Benjamin. At times, I know I've let them shield me from opportunities through which I might have grown. Mistrusting some of my teachers and employers, prospective boyfriends and mentors, I've kept my distance to protect myself from the exploitation or betrayals I feared would come. I've surely misjudged some persons, been too cautious. At other times, my instincts for self-protection have been on target. In second grade, for example, a long-term substitute teacher (whose name I no longer remember) often chose me as errand girl, because I was, according to her repeated statements, the only student who finished my class work neatly and correctly. Although the job was an honor, after a while I didn't like being singled out. My regular teacher, Mrs. White, who was away on maternity leave, had let everybody have a turn, and she hadn't praised one student in ways designed to make others feel inadequate. When my father suggested I take roses and peonies from our garden to the new teacher, I did so reluctantly. In the following weeks, she continued to praise me, but she also punished me for getting some of my morning arithmetic problems wrong, hitting my printing hand hard with a ruler once for every mistake I'd made. I rebelled. One morning when she asked me to read aloud during group time, I would not consent, explaining, "My mother told me not to talk in school." The class came to a halt, with the substitute calling for the principal, who called for my mother to report to the school at once. Although my mother and the principal, Mrs. Thornton, got me to agree to participate in the class, in a few days the teacher had been replaced.

I'm still amazed when I see myself as that skinny, reserved little girl, using my quiet voice and my silence to cause trouble. According to my mother, Mrs. Thornton, who'd taught my sister Joyce years before, realized that my willfulness was just one sign of how the teacher's rigidity and insensitivity had inspired alienation and silence in my formerly enthusiastic class. I was lucky my principal understood that my and my classmates' resistant behavior were responses to a teacher's misguided attempts to control us. My act of aggressive passivity led not to my punishment, but rather to change that benefited me and my friends. I can only hope that if my strong-willed son misbehaves, for whatever reason, that his educators will be as caring, insightful, and flexible as Mrs. Thornton was.

At Benjamin's school, he has long been known as "a gentle soul" and as a child with model behavior, playing well singly and with friends, not using violence to express anger or frustration, cleaning up after himself, and following the teachers' rules. Yet I wonder about what happens when Benjamin starts making public his not-so-sensitive-and-gentle side, when he shows how demanding and self-interested and angry and dismissive he can be. At home my husband David and I accept him as a very vocal, self-assertive, resourceful child, who likes to do things his way and who often ignores our familiar directions and warnings. When Benjamin was small, his principal caretaker often commented that "Ben doesn't cry much. He's such a contented baby, until he sees you two coming." He'd often express his need for love and attention, as well as the frustrations he'd held in while in daycare, by yelling at us and making trouble. I know this behavioral pattern is common among young children. I know it's a truism that parents wouldn't want a paid caretaker, especially one with more than one child on her hands, to have to endure all the feelings babies share with parents. Yet I also know that even the most well-behaved children need to learn how to show more than a pretty or handsome or clever picture of themselves. And I want Benjamin to be able to show his fullness and to speak and sing in his many voices.

In the last couple of weeks, Benjamin has twice spoken with me about some of his voices. On the first occasion, when we were alone together kneading Play Dough in the kitchen, he told me, "Mommy, you know, I have two voices. I can let you hear them both now, if you like." He said one simple sentence in a clear, quiet, hesitant voice and then another sentence in the same clear, quiet, hesitant voice. He looked at me calmly and I asked, "Are those your voices, Benjamin? All your voices?" And he said, "Yes, Mommy. Two." A few days ago, though he still had two voices, he could "only use one." On both occasions, I thought to myself, but Benjamin, you have so many others. I wasn't sure I should say this, however, because he seemed so proud that he could share those he was admitting to. Yet I thought of the various voices he adopts, that express confidence, fear, confusion, happiness, and indecision. There are the gravelly voices, alone, each expressing a different kind of self-assurance—for instance, the one in which he describes a process—the way a backhoe lets out its legs (to secure itself to a surface), scoops up dirt, and drops it into a dump truck, or the way he made Spritz cookies or cornbread with his Aunt Joyce. And there's a range of smoother tones that signal his cool self-assurance, even smugness, for instance, that he used with his twenty-two-month-old cousin James this past Thanksgiving in St. Louis. A native of the Bronx, whom we see only once a year, James seemed to idolize Benjamin, toddling around in his tracks, trying to touch every toy that interested Benjamin, and earning praise for calling out "Ben," as they played with cars and trains. At one point, my son looked up from his Matchbox car, gave James a quick glance, and said, after his Aunt Lisa complimented James on yet another use of "Ben," "Now try Benjamin."

That cool tone brings to mind another moment in which self-assurance was mixed with anxiety and fear, a moment when Benjamin's self-confidence seemed more hard-won and more gratifying, a moment perhaps characteristic of some of the challenges Benjamin will face. At daycare, when Ben was making the transition from a room with young toddlers to one with two-year-olds, he feared my leaving and would cling to me tearfully no matter how long I stayed to comfort him. I worked out a ritual that included reading him two or three books before I kissed and hugged him goodbye and led him to the teacher, who comforted him as I left. Benjamin would refuse to interact with the other children in the room, but they defied his desire for quiet time with me by crowding around as I read him his copy of *Ten Apples Up On Top* and other books he would choose from the room library. One morning only one child, Katie K., came near, and she announced, "Ben's afraid of me." As Benjamin stood and I kneeled before her, I told her I didn't think so, and explained that he just had to get used to being in the midst of so much activity after being alone with his dad and me at home. Then she said, "He can't talk." I said, "Yes, he can. He talks, but he's shy." Benjamin chimed in, "And I got two books. I got books." Though I really liked Katie, I thought, "He told you." I suppose I could be making too much of this exchange, but I saw it as a kind of declaration of independence. Katie had acted as Benjamin's "play mother" before she had graduated to the two-year-olds' room he was just entering, treating him as if he were a little doll (when he was the youngest and smallest child in the room). Yet here he was presenting himself as a holder and counter of books, as bibliophile (thus, connected with his parents' work, which is teaching and writing about books), and as one who could prove another wrong through his manipulation of words. He presented himself tentatively but persuasively as his own (little) man.

Benjamin sometimes asks me about Daddy, usually with hesitance because he knows that Daddy died some time in the past. Benjamin isn't comfortable with people and things that have died. But I'm beginning to tell him about ways he is like Daddy and about the ways our relationship is like that between Daddy and me. When Benjamin helps me make banana bread or biscuits, I tell him that Daddy used to help me stir up pound cakes, and that I'll teach him how to do so, too, if he likes. When Benjamin, fresh from finishing a painting on his new easel, calls out that he's an artist "just like my Aunt Joyce," I sometimes remind him that his grandfather was (and Uncle Houston still is) an artist, too. I also like to tell Benjamin, that just as he likes to listen to my stories, Daddy shared stories with me. One day I'll try to recreate one of them for Benjamin, and I know it will register Daddy's and Benjamin's voices, as well as my own.

Alice Walker

Brothers and Sisters

We lived on a farm in the South in the fifties, and my brothers, the four of them I knew (the fifth had left home when I was three years old), were allowed to watch animals being mated. This was not unusual; nor was it considered unusual that my older sister and I were frowned upon if we even asked, innocently, what was going on. One of my brothers explained the mating one day, using words my father had given him: "The bull is getting a little something on his stick," he said. And he laughed. "What stick?" I wanted to know. "Where did he get it? How did he pick it up? Where did he put it?" All my brothers laughed.

I believe my mother's theory about raising a large family of five boys and three girls was that the father should teach the boys and the mother teach the girls the facts, as one says, of life. So my father went around talking about bulls getting something on their sticks and she went around saying girls did not need to know about such things. They were "womanish" (a very bad way to be in those days) if they asked.

The thing was, watching the matings filled my brothers with an aimless sort of lust, as dangerous as it was unintentional. They knew enough to know that cows, months after mating, produced calves, but they were not bright enough to make the same connection between women and their offspring.

Sometimes, when I think of my childhood, it seems to me a particularly hard one. But in reality, everything awful that happened to me didn't seem to happen to me at all, but to my older sister. Through some incredible power to negate my presence around people I did not like, which produced invisibility (as well as an ability to appear mentally vacant when I was nothing of the kind), I was spared the humiliation she was subjected to, though at the same time, I felt every bit of it. It was as if she suffered for my benefit, and I vowed early in my life that none of the things that made existence so miserable for her would happen to me.

The fact that she was not allowed at official matings did not mean she never saw any. While my brothers followed my father to the mating pens on the other side of the road near the barn, she stationed herself near the pigpen, or followed our many dogs until they were in a mating mood, or, failing to witness something there, she watched the chickens. On a farm it is impossible not to be conscious of sex, to wonder about it, to dream . . . but to whom was she to speak of her feelings? Not to my father, who thought all young women perverse. Not to my mother, who pretended all her children grew out of stumps she magically found in the forest. Not to me, who never found anything wrong with this lie.

When my sister menstruated she wore a thick packet of clean rags between her legs. It stuck out in front like a penis. The boys laughed at her as she served them at the table. Not knowing any better, and because our parents did not dream of actually *discussing* what was going on, she would giggle nervously at herself. I hated her for giggling, and it was at those times I would think of her as dim-witted. She never complained, but she began to have strange fainting fits whenever she had her period. Her head felt as if it were splitting, she said, and everything she ate came up again. And her cramps were so severe she could not stand. She was forced to spend several days of each month in bed.

My father expected all of his sons to have sex with women. "Like bulls," he said, "a man *needs* to get a little something on his stick." And so, on Saturday nights, into town they went, chasing the girls. My sister was rarely allowed into town alone, and if the dress she wore fit too snugly at the waist, or if her cleavage dipped too far below her collarbone, she was made to stay home.

"But why can't I go too," she would cry, her face screwed up with the effort not to wail.

"They're boys, your brothers, *that's* why they can go."

Naturally, when she got the chance, she responded eagerly to boys. But when this was discovered she was whipped and locked up in her room.

I would go in to visit her.

"Straight Pine,"[1] she would say, "you don't know what it *feels* like to want to be loved by a man."

"And if this is what you get for feeling like it I never will," I said, with—I hoped—the right combination of sympathy and disgust.

"Men smell so good," she would whisper ecstatically. "And when they look into your eyes, you just melt."

Since they were so hard to catch, naturally she thought almost any of them terrific.

"Oh, that Alfred!" she would moon over some mediocre, square-headed boy, "he's so *sweet!*" And she would take his ugly picture out of her bosom and kiss it.

My father was always warning her not to come home if she ever

---

1 A pseudonym.

found herself pregnant. My mother constantly reminded her that abortion was a sin. Later, although she never became pregnant, her period would not come for months at a time. The painful symptoms, however, never varied or ceased. She fell for the first man who loved her enough to beat her for looking at someone else, and when I was still in high school, she married him.

My fifth brother, the one I never knew, was said to be different from the rest. He had not liked matings. He would not watch them. He thought the cows should be given a choice. My father had disliked him because he was soft. My mother took up for him. "Jason is just tenderhearted," she would say in a way that made me know he was her favorite; "he takes after me." It was true that my mother cried about almost anything.

Who was this oldest brother? I wondered.

"Well," said my mother, "he was someone who always loved you. Of course he was a great big boy when you were born and out working on his own. He worked on a road gang building roads. Every morning before he left he would come in the room where you were and pick you up and give you the biggest kisses. He used to look at you and just smile. It's a pity you don't remember him."

I agreed.

At my father's funeral I finally "met" my oldest brother. He is tall and black with thick gray hair above a young-looking face. I watched my sister cry over my father until she blacked out from grief. I saw my brothers sobbing, reminding each other of what a great father he had been. My oldest brother and I did not shed a tear between us. When I left my father's grave he came up and introduced himself. "You don't ever have to walk alone," he said, and put his arms around me.

One out of five ain't too bad, I thought, snuggling up.

But I didn't discover until recently his true uniqueness: He is the only one of my brothers who assumes responsibility for all his children. The other four all fathered children during those Saturday-night chases of twenty years ago. Children—my nieces and nephews whom I will probably never know—they neither acknowledge as their own, provide for, or even see.

It was not until I became a student of women's liberation ideology that I could understand and forgive my father. I needed an ideology that would define his behavior in context. The black movement had given me an ideology that helped explain his colorism (he *did* fall in love with my mother partly because she was so light; he never denied it). Feminism helped explain his sexism. I was relieved to know his sexist behavior was not something uniquely his own, but, rather, an imitation of the behavior of the society around us.

All partisan movements add to the fullness of our understanding of society as a whole. They never detract; or, in any case, one must not allow them to do so. Experience adds to experience. "The more things the better," as O'Connor and Welty both have said, speaking, one of marriage, the other of Catholicism.

I desperately needed my father and brothers to give me male models I could respect, because white men (for example; being particularly handy in this sort of comparison)—whether in films or in person—offered man as dominator, as killer, and always as hypocrite.

My father failed because he copied the hypocrisy. And my brothers—except for one—never understood they must represent half the world to me, as I must represent the other half to them.[2]

---

2 Since this essay was written, my brothers have offered their name, acknowledgment, and some support to all their children.

Gerald Early

A Racial Education, Part Two

"The black kids at school are stupid," Rosalind said angrily as she slammed the door coming home from school one day.

"How so?" I asked, curious about this outburst.

"Do you know what they said to me today? They said I must be biracial, that one of my parents must be white," she said, totally confounded.

"Why do they believe that?" I inquired.

"Because of the way I talk. They say I sound like a white person, so one of my parents must be white. They're so stupid. What am I supposed to do? Talk like them? Go around cursing all the time or saying 'y'all' and 'ain't' and stuff like that? Is that supposed to be the way black people talk? I know you and Mommy and your black friends, and the black people at church, and none of you guys talk like that. What am I supposed to sound like, a rap record? I don't like being called white. I'm not white and I'm not biracial. I think they're just ignorant."

I tried to explain to Rosalind that both I and my sisters, when we were children, were often told the same thing. I suggested that perhaps she was overreacting, taking the kids' remarks too seriously. Although, as I remember the remarks of the children when I was little, I thought it strange because the persons I most wanted to sound like were Sidney Poitier (after each time I saw a Sidney Poitier movie I would try to imitate how he walked, how he held his hands, the inflections of his voice) and my grade school teacher, Mr. Lloyd R. King, and I doubt if my sisters had anyone white in mind either: "Jerry and them sound just like white people, all educated and everything," the black kids of the neighborhood would say.

"When black kids told me that when I was young, it was a kind of perverse, left-handed compliment," I said to Rosalind. "They thought you were educated, that you were smart. It's a shame they associate being educated with being white, but that's the way it was and, I guess, still is. But you should try to reach out to them more. I'm sure they didn't mean to insult you when they told you that."

This led Rosalind to a sort of general criticism. "Some of the black kids are okay. But some, especially the boys, act crazy. They're always acting up in class, in the lunchroom, always going to see the principal."

"But you must remember," I replied to Rosalind, "a lot of these kids have severe problems, and for many, busing isn't an easy experience. Besides, not everyone has had your advantages." (This does not seem, in retrospect, so *foolish* a thing to say to a child as it seems a terribly over-measured adult thing to say. In the end, Necile the nymph is right when she tells Santa Claus in L. Frank Baum's *The Life and Adventures of Santa Claus:* "Riches are like a gown which may be put on or taken away, leaving the child unchanged." Nothing touches a child so much as the other humans of which it partakes and with whom it bonds. And so what I said to Rosalind shows how far removed we parents can be from what our children understand.)

Both my wife and I have tried, a bit halfheartedly I must admit, a number of ventures to help our children "relate to their blackness," so to speak, because the problem with black friends grows, I would guess, from how my children understand what being black is. There is a certain contradictory frenzy, a conflicted sloth, to all of this.

"I'm tired of all this race stuff," Ida said to me once, exasperated by it all. "Why do black people always have to carry around a race burden? I want my children to be able to eat, go to the bathroom, and sleep, live their lives without always having to think that a Negro is doing it or to care what other black folk are doing."

"Maybe your survival depends upon your race consciousness," I ventured.

"My survival doesn't depend on any such damn thing," Ida snapped back. "And neither does my sanity. But there are a lot of herd-instinct, cowardly, crab-in-a-basket Negroes and some do-good liberal whites who want you to think that."

But it was Ida who led the way with her membership in Jack and Jill, a black organization, run by mothers, whose sole purpose is to get together black, middle-class children who are estranged from each other because, alas, of integration. My wife was particularly up for this at one time because she was a bit chary about the possibility that our daughters might date white boys when they reached dating age. Linnet, in recent years, has been coming home talking about how much she likes white movie stars like Christian Bale and Christian Slater, and she even had a crush on a white schoolmate for a time.

"What's the big deal?" Rosalind said to me once. "There are two black girls at school who date white boys. Who cares?"

"Well, I guess this is a new day and age," I said, laughing.

"Yeah, Daddy, get with the program. You still think the covers of those Mandingo books are hot stuff."

"My daughter, the comedian," I quipped. "Who writes your material? Or are you actually responsible for it all on your own?"

It is, indeed, the prospect of interracial dating that, for the most part, brings the women of Jack and Jill together. Although I am less concerned about interracial dating than some other black parents I know, not because I do not think it is a possibility for my children but because I am more inclined to let them find happiness wherever they can, I cannot say that I am entirely at ease with it. What I object to in "interracial relationships" is some black person's being convinced that he or she cannot possibly date another black person because there is none who is worthy—indeed, being drawn to white simply for snobbish or status reasons. This seems to me to be just another expression of internalized inferiority. I do not mind if my daughters marry whites, but I would feel deeply distressed if I felt this had happened because they thought whites to be superior to the blacks they knew. Perhaps this is why their having black friends is important—nay, essential, according to Ida's thinking for a time— to their well-being. She firmly believed, as she told me, that black Americans cannot face whites as equals, comfortable in a common culture and sharing a common set of terms and values, if they feel that their own group has nothing to offer, provides no sense of who or what they are. But she didn't believe that very deeply or for very long, in fact.

My wife's ventures with Jack and Jill did not work out well for two reasons: First, she thought it was an imposition that only women were allowed to participate in the organization. "We need couples in this, so the burden does not have to be only on one parent. Most of these black women in the group work, just like me, so why the heck do they run an organization as if they were middle-class white women sitting at home?"

Second, Rosalind and Linnet did not like "the events" they

attended, or at least, did not like the company they were forced to keep. The kids "were worse than the black kids at school," Linnet said. "These kids aren't bad, they're bratty. Besides, all of this is so fake, so false. What do we have in common except we're black yuppie kids?"

"That should be enough," I said.

"Well, it isn't," Linnet said with finality. "Are you friends with people just because they're professors?" Contrived? Linnet was right. It was, although whites often bring their children together purely for such social purposes. This was something my daughters did not or could not understand and appreciate. In any case, they did not profit from it the way some of the other children did.

Naturally, as a college professor who runs a black-studies program, my house is filled to the rafters with books by and about black people. I probably own more such books than virtually anyone else in St. Louis. I am not Afrocentric. I do not celebrate "African" ceremonies, so African-American culture is not "demonstrated" in my house. But hardly a week goes by when I do not engage Ida in serious discussion about some aspect of African American culture or politics. Yet there is, with rare exception, something dispassionate, detached, something that seems curiously without the intensity of identification. My children are awash in exposure to African-American culture. They know what the Harlem Renaissance is, who Countee Cullen was, who Miles Davis and Thelonious Monk were. But this has little emotional impact on them—perhaps because there is little emotional impact of any of this knowledge on me. I have taken them, on several occasions, to Afrocentric bookstores, or allowed them to order anything they wish from Afrocentric catalogues.

"Do I have to buy something, Daddy?" Rosalind asks. "I will if it makes you happy. But I really don't want anything."

"Why? I understand the black kids at school wear Malcolm X shirts and stuff like that. I thought you might want something like that, too."

"No, I don't like that stuff that the black kids wear," Linnet says. "They're these Africa-crazy kids and they hate me. They go around wearing these Mother Africa shirts and stuff like that. They call me and Ros Oreos and everything. But in history class they couldn't even name any countries in Africa when the teacher asked. I was naming bunches and bunches of countries from the stuff I read here at home. But they didn't know anything, yet they want to think they're so black. I don't want anything to do with them or wear anything they wear. I'm black and I'm not ashamed of it. And I don't need a shirt to tell anybody I'm black or to tell anybody I'm not ashamed. All I have to do is live my life the way I want to."

And in a way I was relieved to hear her say this: the commodification of African-American politics and culture, through the low-brow and middle-brow impulses of Afrocentrism, strikes me not as a solution to the problem of black identity, but simply a capitulation to the larger problem of what it means to be an American. For many Americans, it means precisely what one can buy and consume, and an identity, political or otherwise, becomes just another sign of status, a billboard of falsely conceived pride mixed with a hotly induced resentment, not the hard-fought realization of the complexities of consciousness.

"You could just play along with them," I said.

"I don't want to play along with people who don't want to accept me for what I am," Linnet said sharply.

One night, we sat in a circle on the floor and I read to them Etheridge Knight's famous poem, "The Idea of Ancestry." They were silent for a while after hearing it. Then they wanted to know if Etheridge Knight was really in prison when he wrote the poem and if he was really a drug addict.

Suddenly, Rosalind blurted out: "I don't like that poem. Are you trying to tell us something about being black, Daddy? Well, I don't care. I don't like that poem." Then she rose and left the room. I turned to Linnet.

"What did you think?" I asked.

"I liked it," Linnet said. "I thought it was a nice poem. Are you mad Ros didn't like it?"

"No," I said, "not at all. She is entitled to like or dislike whatever she chooses."

"Will you ask her why she didn't like it?"

"No," I said thoughtfully. "She has her reasons. Let's leave it at that."

Just as suddenly Rosalind reentered the room, carrying a book: "Read this," she said, then as an afterthought, shyly, "if you don't mind." It was a copy of some children's poems by Robert Louis Stevenson.

I took the book, Rosalind retook her place on the floor, and I began to read.

E. Ethelbert Miller

Fathering Words

I.

A child born on Good Friday is God's child. An old woman told my mother she was blessed for giving birth to Richard on the day Jesus died. Maybe this is just another story I remember hearing in Brooklyn after piano lessons. I don't know. Richard was my big brother. Long before black men would pass each other in the street and give strange handshakes, or simply nod in solidarity, I had a brother I was in love with. It was Richard whose spirit filled our house. His knowledge of classical music, Latin, animals, and sculpture gave color to our lives in the Bronx. It was my brother who now and then mentioned that he wanted to be pope. Dressed in sheets, blankets, or bathrobes, Richard knew how to part the Red Sea, feed the hungry, and be more holy than all the characters in those television movies shown around the Christmas holiday.

In his room, he built an altar. Two tall candles stood on each end. On the wall a large wooden crucifix. My father claimed it fell from the wall the day Richard returned from the monastery. I can believe it, because something died inside my brother when he returned home from upstate New York. His head had been shaven by monks. What a surprise to come back from the grocery store and find my brother and father laughing like old friends. What secrets were they sharing? I stood between my sister and mother, separated from the men in my family.

I guess it started around the corner, behind the doors of St. Margaret Episcopal Church. Richard was an altar boy who held incense and candles for Father Kruger. The organ music would touch the top of the ceiling and press against the stained-glass windows. The Bible stories were better than cartoons and Dell comics before Marvel pushed them aside with the Metal Men. Somewhere between J.H.S. 52 and Morris High School, Richard would catch the faith like a cold. He joined the Catholic Church and ran the streets with his friend Ignacio. Ignacio was from Cuba and his family must have left the country when Fidel came to power. I would not even think about this until much later. My brother meanwhile was reading the writings of Thomas Merton in much the same manner as Julius Lester and Ernesto Cardenal. Around the world men were listening to their inner voices, leaving homes for solitude and the embracement of degrees of grace.

While I pulled on my brother's ears, something was tugging at his spirit. Although we were very close, Richard and I did none of the things brothers did. He hated sports and so we could not talk about whether Roberto Clemente was better than Willie Mays, or whether Warren Spahn threw a spitter. My brother was simply not interested. In many ways he reminded me of my father, except for his love of literature. It was Richard who borrowed and failed to return so many library books from the Hunts Point Library, that they sent an employee one Saturday to our home on Longwood Avenue. I answered the door and said I knew no one by the name of Richard Miller. My mother overheard my lie and made me search the house for books. Was this the first time I betrayed my brother?

II.

My brother never talked to me about religion. Maybe it was because I was a girl who had no intention of becoming a nun. I saw many nuns in our neighborhood. You could see them around Fordham Road and Grand Concourse. Karen, my best friend, said the nuns could not dance; they didn't know how to move their bodies. She said the reason they prayed all day was because they could not dance. Not even to the twist and Chubby Checker. What would heaven be like without Sam Cooke and Percy Sledge?

Richard wanted to be a dancer. He liked ballet but my father said only girls danced that way and no son of his was going to wear tights in public. You would be called a he/she if you did. I asked my mother why Richard couldn't do what he wanted. She had no answer or explanations.

I thought Richard's room was strange with the altar and everything. I was always afraid of the candles and the fire. In his closet my brother kept his church robes. I liked the feel of them, the touch of silk on my flesh. Is this what Jesus wore? If he did a woman would believe in him. What a man wears can tell a woman many things. I thought my brother was becoming different from the person I chased in the Bronx Zoo. When we were seven and five and even ten and twelve we were very close. We shared everything, toys, books, and clothes. But one day my brother became holy. There was no halo around his head or even a new look in his eyes. Richard just started reading more and playing the piano constantly. So maybe it was the music after all. When my brother refused to save his money to purchase records, that's when he cut himself off from the rest of us. He listened to that classical stuff. White music is what we called it.

Karen and I thought the stuff was boring. It would make you dance funny or maybe not dance at all. It was the music that trapped my brother. Handel's Messiah *was like a drug. What could you call Mozart and Bach? Richard would pretend he was a conductor and wave his hands in the air. My father encouraged my brother to pursue his love of music, even while his own head was filled with jazz. On the shelf in his closet would be those funny hats, the kind Ethelbert claimed Monk wore before he stopped talking. Leave it to my little brother to find something black in all this. Now that Richard and my father are both dead, it doesn't matter who influenced whom. I just wished I knew them better. All I have are stories and some of them might not even be true. Maybe my brother never became a monk. Maybe he was sent to reform school somewhere in upstate New York. I would like to think he didn't want to leave me. I was his sister and when we were young we were supposed to get married. Monks can't have wives. Didn't Richard know? Why did he lie and not tell me the truth? Why did he not confess? I was so angry with him when our family came back from LaGuardia Airport. My father had to go to work that day. My mother was so sad she didn't even go into the kitchen to fix his lunch. Instead I could hear her crying in the bedroom. I told my baby brother to stop making noise. He was too little to understand what had happened. Richard was gone. The same thing happened after his funeral.*

III.

Just before spring the first flowers bloom. They are beautiful yet very much alone. Like sentries they stand between seasons. This is how I think of my brother as I write *Fathering Words*. It is a warm February day and the earth is drying after a week of rain. I carry a few garbage bags out to the alley behind my house. In my backyard, the presence of white, yellow, and purple buds join with the sounds of birds and the touch of a soft breeze. It is early morning, a Sunday, and I have the money in my pocket to purchase a newspaper. I will take a short walk and stop at a nearby store. My wife and children are asleep and so it is only me and these first flowers that try to speak to each other.

Sometimes a thing of beauty will remind me of my brother. Once it was just how the water of a river ran across the rocks in its bed. I stopped to look from a bridge and felt the enormous amount of grief pouring out from deep inside. This was just a few years ago, so the healing continues. The flowers appear and disappear like all things of beauty.

I never thought my brother would leave me. He never said anything about becoming a monk. Who did he talk to? My father? Mother? I don't remember any conversations during dinner. There were no brochures like the ones you get from the Army and Air Force, on tables around the apartment. Please join God and see the world. No, my brother's departure was as sudden as someone's death. He put on his suit and tie and packed a bag. We got in the Dodge and went to the airport. We waved and came back home.

It was the early sixties and Richard was going north. In the South, the Civil Rights movement was at its peak. Young men and women were struggling to change America. A young James Baldwin spoke of love and fire. My brother left behind a copy of *Giovanni's Room* in his bookcase. My mother let me move my things into his room. The space, however, would remain Richard's during his entire stay at the monastery. I guess my mother knew he was coming back. No one else did. Everything was normal in our house even as outside the nation was being torn apart. What happens to families during civil wars? How do they fight and continue to love? Love and continue to fight?

Did my brother rebel against our parents? Was there an argument that I missed? Were they supportive of him because this was his dream, to become a monk? Did my father simply accept my brother's decision as a bad card given to him from the bottom of the deck? You grow up without a father and then you lose your son. Nothing but a bad joke. The bitterness could force the strongest man to mumble and turn his back on everything. I guess because my father didn't expect much in life it was easy for him to go to work every day without complaint. Or maybe it was the inner spirit, the contemplative soul who looks out the window and wonders about the meaning of life. If one is left alone, the purpose of life is supposed to become as clear as looking at flowers bloom.

My life consists of a medley of schools, P.S. 39 followed by the harsh rhythms of J.H.S. 120 (Paul Laurence Dunbar), Christopher Columbus High School, Howard University, UNLV, Emory & Henry College, Bennington College, and American University. A strange set of cloisters. Each place a step away from 938 Longwood Avenue in the Bronx. In the shadows of my father and brother, I grew for many years quietly in the shade like a vine reaching for daylight. In many ways I created myself. I learned from my father and brother the many ways to disguise sadness and loneliness.

I grew up without a room, a space to call my own. I was given the hallway closet for my books and toys. I had only one or two friends. Dinky and Judy. We played baseball even in winter when there was snow on the ground. Dinky was rumored to be a cousin. His family lived upstairs and members would sometimes come into our apartment without knocking. So I guess we were all related. We knew people who had accents and talked about the West Indian islands as if they were places in the Bible. Judy was my girlfriend and she was Chinese. Her cousin Eva's family operated a laundry not far from school. My early writing consisted of love letters to Judy with my name and a few questions. Do you love me? I love you. Judy's replies would be the only statement I would get in writing until Michelle stopped me on the campus of Howard and asked for directions to the bookstore.

Maybe I should have been given away when I was a child. I could have been raised in Brooklyn, or Queens. Someplace with a backyard and green grass. My room would be the attic. Sun would come in and dance the way my sister did. My family was working class. We had no contact with the black middle class except when we went to see Auntie, my great aunt who lived on what was once called Sugar Hill. Years later the black history courses I took and the books I read would provide a map to the discoveries during my childhood years. I was the type of child who read books, did poorly in math, excellent in social studies, and was the second fastest runner in my class. Throughout my life I was always the runner-up. Second place. Silver medal. No gold or endorsements.

To my mother and father it was Richard who was the son. I was the third child, like a third strike chasing the corner of the plate. A sudden surprise. Everyone is caught looking at the new addition to the family. On occasions when we visited Brooklyn as a family, to join relatives who still had their accents, someone would say to my mother, "Enid, when did you have another child?" This would usually cause some laughter throughout the room. My mother seldom said anything. It was as if the joke was the reminder of a botched abortion.

Both of my parents were always excited about what my brother did. It must have started with his first baby steps and words. I can see my brother crawling around on the floor with my father taking pictures. Richard was the handsome child, his hair different from my own as well as Marie's. It was Richard my father wanted to show off to the world.

A man walks along a beach, turns around, and notices his footsteps for the first time. This is how I can best describe my father as a new father. Richard, his firstborn, a dream he has no problem waking up to feed.

Today I was thinking about the responsibilities of fatherhood. I have never worked a day as hard as my father. If my shoulder or back hurts, it is from spending too many hours at the computer. It does not come from lifting boxes and packages, sorting mail, trying to catch a train in the wee hours of the morning. My father walked down dark streets with his money tucked away in a secret place. How many times was he stopped, robbed, or had his life threatened? As I write *Fathering Words,* I think of my own life, so much different from my father's. Is it a result of mastering the word? Is this what Frederick Douglass realized? The discovery of reading and writing can be linked to freedom.

I live a writer's life, surrounded by books, ideas, and yes, dreams. What I am doing right now is trying to describe my footsteps. How did I get here? What did I discover as well as lose along the way? I had a conversation with my agent yesterday about what this book was going to be. "Where was the narrative?" she asked. People need a straight narrative. I thought of the flowers blooming in my backyard. How they suddenly appeared one day after the rain. Their petals flutter in the wind. How sad they look when the weather changes, the cold air encouraging them to return to the earth.

I want to reclaim memory, to feel the ground beneath my feet. The telling of this story must be woven like a quilt. The parts taken from the past, present, and future. The words exist all at once. The life of my brother, father, and I are small patches resting next to each other. This is what I thought when I stood looking at their graves a few years ago. Men reduced to ashes, pieces of men becoming memories. It is the word, the tale, the story that survives. It is the combination of history and myth that creates this book.

I am inside my father's dream. We are coming to America. This will be our beginning. Even before I am born I search for words, for a consciousness. I cross the water with a man who will one day let me breathe. These words today splash against the rocks of time. Each wave returns me to the past and pulls me toward the future. The making of this quilt is like embracing an ocean. How can I wrap my arms around so much water?

Kalamu ya Salaam

Spirit Family of the Streets

Sometimes you don't hear them until they come swinging 'round the corner, off St. Philip turning onto Treme, headed downtown. Sometimes you be on the telephone and have to cut short your conversation so you can run outside and find out who died or what's being celebrated. Usually it's during the light of day but sometimes it's in the heat of the night when you bop out your door and down your concrete steps to slip into the surging sea of revelers streaming joyously down the street. In New Orleans, seems like *sometimes* could be any time for the jump up of a second-line. This fertile crescent has got to be the dancing-est city in America.

I cannot remember ever dancing in a second-line without greeting someone I knew, even if I only knew them by face and not by name. Whether you're next to the bass drum, behind the trombones, or before the trumpet, you always see someone to greet and smile at (or smile with) as they squat down and back up their thang, or pogo bounce on one leg carving a sacred circle in the air, or leap like a Masai in time to the syncopated cross-rhythms echo-echo-echoing off the wooden fences of dilapidated-but-brightly-painted shotgun houses built right up close to these sidewalks that skirt our narrow streets.

You can live miles away and still find your sister's husband snapping pictures with his Nikon, or your brother's oldest girlchild and her best-est buddy strutting their stuff in their checkered, blue-plaid trousers that are the public school uniform. Indeed, isn't that your mama's baby brother who got arthritis, tapping his cane in time to the beat, standing on the corner by the sweet shop? And you are for sure in the house of our holy-togetherness if you went to public or Catholic high school with some of these people, or maybe danced with their sisters at the ILA Hall, the Municipal Auditorium, the State Palace Theatre—or was it on Claiborne and Orleans two Mardi Gras ago? Within this multihued gathering of shaking flesh, it's a given that someone will greet/touch you with a hug, a kiss, or at the very least an enthusiastic pound of fist atop fist.

There are a lot of theories, but no certainties as to the origin of the term *second-line*, but for sure it refers to dancing in the street with a go-for-broke, unabashed shimmy shake ecstasy. What would make a thirty-eight-year-old schoolteacher get "ratty," hike up her skirt and deftly wave a white handkerchief behind her protruding buttocks with nary an ounce of shame in her game? Nothing but the spirit; and when the spirit say groove, you got to move.

In New Orleans, dance traditions are stronger than so-called "social decorum." Here it is customary to prance in the streets while exhibiting a profound interest and demonstrable proficiency in overtly sexual body movements. But that's only logical—there can be no family if there is no sex; therefore, shouldn't we celebrate the family's creation? Even in the midst of grieving the death of a loved one, we dance our defiance and celebrate the joy of life. That is the ultimate strength of the second-line: even at funerals, it affirms the ongoing existence of the family. Thus, these jiggling humans are a spirit family of the streets.

What is a spirit family? Well, there is the nuclear family of father, mother, and their natural issue. There is an extended family of kin and kind—folk related by circumstance and life struggles. And there is the spirit family, an activity-centered sharing of common cultural values.

What is the nuclear family to ordinary Black people? What does it mean: father, mother, and 2.5 children under one roof? Coming from traditional African societies built on elaborate, extended linkages between each person, what sense does it make to define one's "family" exclusively in nuclear terms? If you had to deal with masters who treated you with less respect than a bale of cotton or a healthy mule; who regarded you at best as $\frac{3}{5}$ human; who bred you like pigs; and who callously and methodically separated offspring from parent, how could you maintain the so-called blessed union of man, woman, and child?

And yet, historical documents indicate that during Reconstruction, Black folk went to extraordinary lengths to identify and find brother, father, sister, mother, husband, wife—all manner of kin. Our interpersonal relationships were always important to us, even when we lacked the social authority to shape and maintain our family structures. For us, family has always been more than the definition of immediate blood. During the first half of the twentieth century, the Black family unit often included children rescued from the harshness of segregation-enforced poverty, and/or children of relatives and friends, and reared them inseparably from the biological brood. It was not uncommon to have adopted cousins, aunts, and uncles. Why was this?

We are more than just twisted responses to slavery; more than a limited range of make-do solutions to inhuman social conditions. More of our existence than has thus far been realized is proactive choice, and not simply reactive settling for the lesser of two evils. Our insistence on constantly creating family is ideological, not pathological. We believe in the beauty of community.

The spirit family of the street has many, many expressions in

New Orleans. The main folk articulation is the Social Aid & Pleasure Club (SA&PC). These groups existed formally—as in dues-paying and rule-book-following organizations with administrative officers—as well as informally, in a grapevine sort of way. They became our burial societies, employment agencies, insurance companies, and institutions where skills and goods were bartered by a money-poor membership that knew that if there was to be a good life for the Black poor in The Big Easy, then we had to pledge allegiance to each other.

The anti-Black terror campaign that enforced the repeal of Reconstruction and introduced the Jim Crow era of Black Codes proved not to be the tomb of Black self-determination—as was hoped for by the racist adherents of American apartheid—but, rather, the funeral pyre from which our spirit families rose, phoenixlike. Our parades declared that, regardless of the strictures of segregation, we could and would take care of ourselves, and do so with panache.

With names that range from the lofty, such as Olympia, to the near sacrilegious, such as Money Wasters, the Social Aid and Pleasure Clubs of New Orleans are institutionalized forms of African secret societies, developed for the expressed purpose of building community ("social"), offering mutual support ("aid"), and indisputably having a good time ("pleasure").

Plessy v. *Ferguson* may have ordained that we could not ride first class on public accommodations, but when we strutted up and down our dusty streets, we declared our independence from American conceptions of who and what so-called "colored people" were. By the twenties, Blacks in New Orleans had reconstructed the course of twentieth-century American culture. Henceforth, American popular culture could not be defined without referring to jazz and Black-inspired dance—indeed, the twenties could not have become the Jazz Age had we not created jazz. And this new music was always accompanied in its hometown by body movement, by dancing, by strutting; even though in most of America the music became a concert tradition played indoors mainly for listening, in New Orleans the street remained the natural venue of spiritual expression.

Each of the SA&PCs has an annual celebration of their ongoing existence. At these events—usually held in autumn—the members step out dressed to the nines, in colors that would rival Romare Bearden's celebrated palette. Shoes that can cost more than half the monthly rent. Hats special-ordered from some obscure merchant in a far-off city. Silk shirts dyed a shockingly vibrant hue. I have seen club members dressed up and standing proudly tall, albeit supported by a walker—they ride the route in the club car (a highly waxed, spit-polished maroon Cadillac borrowed from Big Head Willie, who runs the sandwich shop over on Orleans Avenue). These stalwarts have been paid-up club members for twenty-plus years and, physical infirmities notwithstanding, have to be counted in that number of those present for the kickoff of the perennial parade.

These are poor people for the most part; workers who are systematically underpaid their entire lives. Some may ask what they get out of this. But does anyone ask what does a materially-impoverished but spiritually-empowered mother get out of resplendently dressing her children for church? So what if "Cou-zan Louie" (as cousin Louis is affectionately known in this neighborhood) has been sick? He's part of the family. Even though he has to lean on a walker, Louis nevertheless decisively demonstrates where his heart is at when he shifts his once-legendary dance style from the lower extremities of his youth (wild ass, crossed and uncrossed leg shakes) to the sloping shoulders of his declining years (twitching mischievously in mini-motions that make him look like he has a massive vibrator hidden in the back of his jacket). Louis has metamorphosed his formerly fleet feet into subtle twists and turns of his gray-haired head. His semi-paralyzed, but still vigorous, dance is done with a deft aplomb and twinkling eye that outshines the more athletic achievements of countless younger and healthier people. For "Cou-zan Louie" and thousands like him, there is no doubt that our music is medicinal, and the conviviality of our camaraderie is rejuvenating.

Beyond cementing the community, and keeping alive the spirit of music and dance, the SA&PCs of New Orleans also function as a cultural calabash containing Afrocentric aesthetics and philosophy. To this day, New Orleans remains America's most African city. You cannot live in New Orleans and go untouched by the spiritual, aesthetic, and philosophical power of Blackness. For example, here, even members of the Jewish community use a brass band to accompany the carrying of the sacred Torah during rare outdoor religious ceremonies.

In addition to the SA&PCs, another Afrocentric spiritual franchise is the Mardi Gras Indians, whose exquisitely colored, handcrafted suits honor a tradition of united Black and Red resistance to genocide. Thus the Mardi Gras Indians stress that our new family is broader than some mythological blood purity—mixing, or "miscegenation," was no problem for us. If we could be Black and Blue, if some of us could flaunt our "roon-ness" (quadroon, octoroon, and so forth), then certainly we could, and—given the realities of our history—*should* be Blacks who are not only Blue and partially White, but Red, too! Without ever cracking a sociology book, or doing a statistical genealogical sampling, the Mardi Gras Indians spell out the broad definition of family, a definition that goes deeper than blood, a definition that embraces the spirit of life as it is actually lived, rather than mythologically romanticized.

What is most admirable about the spirit family of the street is that it maintains its sovereignty even when there is a lack of formal structure. There is no government agency directing the second-line; no private sponsorships or aristocratic patrons paying for this out of the treasure chests of their pockets. The second-line does not request permission to exist. We do it because we want to, whenever we want to. It doesn't have to be a warm Sunday when the Treme Sidewalk Steppers are celebrating their anniversary; nor does it have to be Mardi Gras day when the Yellow Pocahontases are outshining the sun. No, it could be an ordinary Wednesday afternoon, partly cloudy and neither hot nor cold, and here they come, drums beating and horns blaring a clarion, centuries-old call: "Get your Black ass on in these streets!" (I have not described the indescribable music that accompanies the second-line, because words don't go there. No words, or musical notes transcribed to a page, can capture the excitement this ancient music generates.) Self-absorbed six-year-olds strut on the corners, convincing themselves they are dancing just like Big Jake—and everybody know can't nobody jook like Big Jake, except maybe Miss Noonay, who got more wicked moves than a Louisiana politician lying under oath; anyway, that's how them kids be dancing.

No television can teach this. No computer can buck jump like this. For, like I said earlier, at the core of this spirit lies a healthy enjoyment of human eros—in our communities no one is ashamed to shake their thing: "This butt is mine, God gave it to me, and I ain't supposed to just sit on it!" And like family always do, we encourage the kids to show off and guffaw uproariously as the elders remind us not only were they once young but, more importantly, they still have some youthful vigor in their aching bones and withered flesh. The second-line is a way not only of celebrating life, but of building the future. The second-line gives young people something to look forward to as they try to do the dances the adults do, and gives elders a future to imagine as they teach their grandchildren to carry on after the current generation is gone.

That is why Mr. Al is standing in the intersection as the second-line makes it on down the street. Sporting a bemused, dimpled smile, Al look like Elegba, a cultural sentry doing his duty at the crossroads. Mr. Al does not go inside until all of the children are safe back on the sidewalks and porches, and the procession has turned another corner. With an unshakable certainty, Al knows that the family that dances together stays together, that music and movement are a form of prayer, that with this spirit in us we will never die, never, and that at moments like this, everything was, is, and will continue to be jelly, jelly, jelly, cause jam don't shake like that.

Let the congregation respond: *aché*.

THE EDITOR

Afaa Michael Weaver (b. Michael S. Weaver) is a veteran of fifteen years as a blue-collar factory worker in his native Baltimore. In 1986, he completed his B.A. at Regents College and, in 1987, his M.F.A. at Brown University. His first book of poetry, *Water Song*, appeared in 1985, and was fol-

lowed by *My Father's Geography* (1992), *Stations in a Dream* (1993), *Timber and Prayer* (1995), *Talisman* (1998), *Multitudes: Poems Selected & New* (2000), *The Ten Lights of God* (2000), and a chapbook, *Sandy Point* (2000). He is the recipient of a National Endowment for the Arts grant, and a fellowship from the Pew Charitable Trusts. In 2002, he was a Fulbright Visiting Scholar at National Taiwan University and Taipei National University of the Arts in Taipei, Taiwan, where he was given the name Wei, Ya-feng, after the Chinese mythological hero from *The Book of Songs*.

Mr. Weaver holds an endowed chair at Simmons College in Boston, where he is Alumnae Professor of English.

CONTRIBUTORS

Tara Betts teaches writing with Young Chicago Authors. She is working on a manuscript of poems about Ida B. Wells-Barnett. Her work has appeared in *Power Lines: A Decade of Poetry from Chicago's Guild Complex, Poetry Slam, Bum Rushin' the Page, Obsidian III, Columbia Poetry Review,* and *That Takes Ovaries!* Her poetry was featured in the Steppenwolf Theater production, *Words on Fire.* In addition to fellowships at Ragdale and Centrum, Tara won the Gwendolyn Brooks Open Mic Award and an Illinois Arts Council Literary Award. Tara represented Chicago in the National Poetry Slam in 1999 and 2000.

Gwendolyn Brooks is the author of many books, including poetry, a novel, writing manuals, and an autobiography. Among her many honors are a Pulitzer Prize, the National Medal of Arts, the American Academy of Arts and Letters Award, Guggenheim Fellowships, the National Endowment for the Arts Lifetime Achievement Award, and from the National Book Foundation, a Medal for Distinguished Contribution to American Letters. The Gwendolyn Brooks Center for Black Literature and Culture, the major resource for information about her life and work, is located at Chicago State University, where she taught as Writer-in-Residence.

Karen Chandler is an associate professor at the University of Louisville, where she teaches courses on African-American literature and film. She has previously published essays on film, literature, and the black vernacular in such journals as *Obsidian III, Arizona Quarterly, The Henry James Review*, and *African American Review*. Much of her academic research grows out of the experience of storytelling she came to know as a child, in which listeners were encouraged to be active shapers of meaning. Her analyses of literary and film texts are informed by her interest in how audiences play with stories' meanings. She is now completing a book on melodramatic narratives and their appeal for black and white women.

Poet and novelist **Fred D'Aguiar** grew up in Guyana and London, England. His *New and Selected Poems*, drawn from four previous collections, appeared in the UK from Chatto and Windus Press in Spring 2001. *Feeding the Ghosts* (Ecco Press, 1999) is his third novel. The Overlook Press published his verse novel, *Bloodlines*, in summer 2001. He is Professor of English and Creative Writing at the University of Miami, Florida, where he has taught since 1995.

Edwidge Danticat was born in Haiti in 1969, and was raised by her aunt under the dictatorial Duvalier regime. She was reunited with her parents and brothers in America when she was twelve. She published her first writings two years later, and holds a degree in literature from Barnard College and an M.F.A. from Brown University. She is the author of two novels—*Breath, Eyes, Memory* (Soho Press, 1994) and *The Farming of Bones* (Soho Press, 1998). Her story collection *Krik? Krak!* was nominated for the National Book Award in 1995. She is the recipient of a James Michener

Fellowship, a Lila Wallace–Reader's Digest Writers' Award, the Italian Flaiano Award, and an American Book Award.

Jarvis Q. DeBerry grew up in northern Mississippi, near the small town of Holly Springs. While studying engineering at Washington University in St. Louis, he failed a mandatory composition test and then decided to major in English in part to prove the test a fluke. He works as an editorial writer at the *Times-Picayune* newspaper in New Orleans and is a member of the NOMMO Literary Society. His work appears in *Cave Canem: V, Step Into a World*, and is scheduled to appear in *Bum Rush the Page: A Def Poetry Jam*.

Gerald Early is the Merle S. King Professor of Modern Letters at Washington University and the author and editor of numerous books on American culture. As an author, his most recent book, *When Worlds Collide: Anxiety, Miscegenation, and American Culture in the 1950s*, is from Harvard University Press (2001). His other books include *One Nation Under a Groove: Motown and American Culture*; *Daughters: On Family and Fatherhood*; and *The Culture of Bruising: Essays on Literature, Prizefighting, and Modern American Culture*, which was the winner of the National Book Critics Circle Award in Criticism. His work as an editor includes *The Muhammad Ali Reader*. He is the recipient of a Whiting Writer's Award and a member of the American Academy of Arts and Sciences. His work has been published in *Harper's*, *The Atlantic Monthly*, and the *Best American Essays* series. He lives in St. Louis.

Lise Funderburg is a Philadelphia-based writer, book critic, and essayist who often looks at issues of community, identity, and race.

Life, in other words. Her collection of rural histories, *Black, White, Other: Biracial Americans Talk About Race and Identity*, was described by the *New York Times Book Review* as "an important book...an example of how we can talk about race with feeling, humor and dignity." Funderburg earned her B.A. in English Literature at Reed College in Portland, Oregon, and her M.A. in Journalism at the Columbia University School of Journalism. She has worked as both writer and editor for a number of national and regional magazines, and is currently a senior writer at *Time* magazine. She is also working on a book about longstanding racially and socio-economically integrated communities in the U.S., and the ways in which their residents do and don't manage to live across lines of race and class. A piece of her research for that book appeared as the article, "Integration Anxiety," in the *New York Times Magazine* in November 1999.

Henry Louis Gates, Jr. is the W.E.B. Du Bois Professor of Humanities and Chair of the Department of Afro-American Studies at Harvard University. He has been the editor of such collections as *Reading Black, Reading Feminist, The Norton Anthology of African-American Literature*, the forty-volume *Schomburg Library of Nineteenth-Century Black Women Writers 1910–1940*, and the series editor of the complete works of Zora Neale Hurston. He is the author of *The Signifying Monkey*, which received the American Book Award, *Figures in Black*, and the memoir *Colored People*, among other books. A staff writer for *The New Yorker*, he lives in Cambridge, Massachusetts.

W. **Warren Harper** was born in Catskill, New York, June 29, 1915, the second of five children, where he grew up in an all-white town. After the film debut of D. W. Griffith's *The Birth of a Nation* (1915), a mob gathered outside the family's residence where Joseph Charles Harper, "Warren's" father, faced down the mob singlehandedly. At the fiftieth anniversary of Warren's high school graduation, he was surrounded by classmates who considered him the outstanding student of the 1934 graduating class. In another era WWH might have attended Syracuse University as a student-athlete, but he enlisted in the Civilian Conservation Corps to help sustain his family at the height of the Depression. It was the first time he'd ever been in the South. He was told by the camp commandant not to drive a truck anywhere near the town of Williamsburg, Virginia. After the CCC, "Warren" sought work in Brooklyn, New York. The highlight of his remembrance is the title of his memoir: *I'm Katherine*. His ambition was to become a writer. While working in the Brooklyn Postal Service he attended St. John's Law School, though he never practiced, moving his family to Los Angeles, in a postal transfer, in 1951. He was the originator of what we now know as "overnight mail" and lives in retirement in Los Angeles. He is the father of the poet Michael S. Harper.

Honorée Fanonne Jeffers's book, *The Gospel of Barbecue* (The Kent State University Press, 2000), was chosen by Lucille Clifton for the 1999 Stan and Tom Wick Prize for Poetry and was a finalist for the 2001 Paterson Poetry Prize. She has won awards from the Rona Jaffe Foundation and the Barbara Deming Memorial Fund for Women, and her work has appeared in several anthologies and journals, including *African American Review, Brilliant Corners, Dark Matter: A Century of Speculative Fiction from the African Diaspora* (Warner/Aspect, 2000), *Identity Lessons: Contemporary Writing About Learning to Be American* (Viking, 1998), *The Massachusetts Review*, and *Obsidian III.*

Trent Masiki, one of three 1995 Hurston/Wright Award winners, holds an M.F.A. in Creative Writing at Emerson College in Boston. His nonfiction has appeared in *Poets & Writers, Black Issues Book Review*, and the journal *Short Story*. His fiction has appeared in *Callaloo, Reform Judaism Magazine, Xavier Review*, and *Obsidian II: Black Literature in Review*. He is an Assistant Professor of English in Worcester, Massachusetts, where he writes and teaches.

E. Ethelbert Miller is a founding member of the Humanities Council of Washington, D.C., and a commissioner for the D.C. Commission on the Arts and Humanities. He has served as a visiting professor at the University of Nevada, Las Vegas; an associate faculty member of Bennington College; and the Jessie Ball DuPont Scholar at Emory & Henry College. Miller has won several honors, including the 1995 O.B. Hardison Jr. Poetry Prize and an honorary doctorate of literature from Emory & Henry College.

Marilyn Nelson's third book, *The Homeplace* (L.S.U. Press), was a finalist for the 1991 National Book Award and won the 1992 Annisfield-Wolf Award. Her fifth book, *The Fields of Praise: New and Selected Poems* (L.S.U. Press), was a finalist for the 1997 National Book Award, the Lenore Marshall Prize, and the PEN/

Winship Award, and it won the 1998 Poets' Prize. A new book, *Carver: A Life in Poems* (Front Street Books) appeared in 2001.

Kalamu ya Salaam is founder of NOMMO Literary Society, a black writers workshop; co-founder of Runagate Multimedia; leader of the WordBand, a poetry performance ensemble; and moderator of CyberDrum, a listserve of over 1000 black writers and ethnically diverse supporters of literature. His latest book is *360°—A Revolution of Black Poets*, edited with Kwame Alexander. Salaam's latest spoken-word CD is *My Story, My Song*.

Della Taylor Scott teaches African-American Fiction and Culture Matters, a writing course for first-year students, at Simmons College in Boston. For the past ten years, she has been the editor of *Abafazi*, a refereed black women's studies journal that is distributed around the globe. Ms. Scott received the Massachusetts Artists Foundation Finalist Award for Fiction and was a nominee for a Pushcart Prize for fiction. Her fiction has been anthologized, and her work has been published in *Callaloo, The Haight Ashbury Literary Journal, JAM*, and *The Writers' Haven Journal*. She is a member of the diversity committee of PEN New England and is at work on a novel and a short story collection.

Alice Walker won the Pulitzer Prize and the American Book Award for her novel *The Color Purple*, which was preceded by *The Third Life of George Copeland* and *Meridian*. Her other bestselling novels include *By the Light of My Father's Smile, Possessing the Secret of Joy*, and *The Temple of My Familiar*. She is also the author of two collections of short stories, three collections of essays, five volumes of poetry, and several children's books. Her books have been translated into more than two dozen languages. Born in Eatonton, Georgia, Walker now lives in Northern California.

ACKNOWLEDGMENTS

Tara Betts. "Peace Offerings" appears here for the first time. Used by permission of the author.

Gwendolyn Brooks. "Keziah" is reprinted from *Report From Part Two* © 1996 by Gwendolyn Brooks. Reprinted by permission of Third World Press, Inc.

Karen Chandler. "Making Noise" appears here for the first time. Used by permission of the author.

Fred D'Aguiar. "A Son in Shadow" first appeared in *Harper's Magazine.*

Edwidge Danticat. "The Future in My Arms" first appeared in the magazine *Ebony.* Reprinted by permission of Edwidge Danticat and the Watkins/Loomis Agency.

Jarvis Q. DeBerry. "Roy DeBerry" appears here for the first time. Used by permission of the author.

Gerald Early. "A Racial Education, Part Two" is reprinted from *Daughters: On Family and Fatherhood* © 1994 by Gerald Early. Used by permission of the author.

Lise Funderburg. "Letter from Monticello" appears here for the first time. Used by permission of the author.

Henry Louis Gates, Jr. "Up the Hill" is reprinted from *Colored People: A Memoir* © 1994 by Henry Louis Gates, Jr. Used by permission of Alfred A. Knopf, a division of Random House, Inc.

W. Warren Harper. "The Matriarch," "Catskill High School," "In Limbo," "Mother," and are reprinted from *I'm Katherine: A Memoir*. Reprinted by permission of the author.

Honorée Fanonne Jeffers. "The Tail of Color" appears here for the first time. Used by permission of the author.

Trent Masiki. "A Curious Absence" appears here for the first time. Used by permission of the author.

E. Ethelbert Miller. Chapter Three is reprinted from *Fathering Words: The Making of an African American Writer* © 2000. Reprinted by permission of the author.

Marilyn Nelson. "My Cleaning Lady" appears here for the first time. Used by permission of the author.

Kalamu ya Salaam. "Spirit Family of the Streets" is an abridged version of an essay reprinted from a photo exhibit catalogue, *The Ties That Bind: Making Family New Orleans Style* © 2000. Reprinted by permission of the author.

Della Taylor Scott. "My Country 'Tis of Thee" appears here for the first time. Used by permission of the author.

Alice Walker. "Brothers and Sisters" is reprinted from *In Search of Our Mothers' Gardens: Womanist Prose* © 1975 by Alice Walker. Reprinted by permission of Harcourt, Inc.

PHOTO CREDITS

Sarah Putnam   page 1

Debbie Dalton   page 29

Joanna Morissey   page 51

Carol Venezia   page 97

Young Chicago Authors   page 161

Nancy Crampton   page 175

Mark Cohen   page 215

Lynda Koolish   page 237